ESSAYS,

&c.

ESSAYS

ON

SOME OF THE PECULIARITIES

OF THE

CHRISTIAN RELIGION.

———

BY

RICHARD WHATELY, D.D.

PRINCIPAL OF ST. ALBAN'S HALL, OXFORD, AND LATE FELLOW
OF ORIEL COLLEGE.

———

OXFORD,

PRINTED BY W. BAXTER,

FOR JOHN MURRAY, LONDON.

1825.

TO THE

RIGHT HONOURABLE

LORD GRENVILLE,

CHANCELLOR OF THE UNIVERSITY OF OXFORD.

———◆———

MY LORD,

THE following work contains the substance of some discourses delivered by me, as Select Preacher, before this University; a place to which I have been long affectionately attached, and for my restoration to which, as a resident member, I am indebted to your Lordship's favour.

It is also the first work I have brought before the public, since my appointment to the situation I now hold.

By inscribing it therefore to your Lordship, I considered that I was adopting the most appropriate mode within my reach, of testifying how sensible I am of the kindness, as well as the honour, implied in this selection.

I could not indeed but feel proud of owing my appointment to a Nobleman, with whom I had no personal or political connexion, and who had always been regarded as the patron of academical merit, as well as a steady promoter of the welfare of the University.

Before I was placed where I now am, it might have exposed me to the suspicion of interested views, if I had offered such a publication to your notice, or ventured to express those sentiments of respect which are common to every member, and to every true friend, of this University: but a dedication to one from whom I have already received all that I could ever hope to obtain, can only be interpreted, I trust, by yourself, and by the world, as a tribute, however humble, of gratitude for a past favour, and of applause for public virtues.

I have the honour to be,

My Lord,

Your Lordship's most obliged

and most obedient humble Servant,

RICHARD WHATELY.

St. Alban's Hall,
Nov. 28, 1825.

PREFACE.

THE greater part of the substance of the following Essays was delivered in several discourses before the University of Oxford, about five years ago. They were not originally designed for publication; but the author was induced to entertain the idea at the suggestion of some friends, whose opinions are entitled to deference, and who thought that the views contained in them might have the effect on some minds, not of introducing new doctrines, but of awakening attention to some important points which are very frequently overlooked; and that the chain of argument would appear to more advantage, and would be likely to be more justly estimated, when comprised in a volume, than when delivered, as was necessarily the case, at long intervals from the University pulpit.

Various avocations, which have delayed the publication of these Essays till the present time, have also had the effect, in some degree, of preventing their receiving that minute examination in every part, and careful correction, which a proper respect both for the subject and for the reader might seem to demand : but as these avocations were not likely either to cease, or to be diminished, it was not thought desirable to keep back the work any longer, in the hope of bestowing on it that undivided attention, which unavoidable obstacles might prevent it from ever receiving.

It is hardly necessary to observe, that I have not entertained the design of noticing *all* the peculiarities of the Christian religion; which would indeed amount to little less than a complete system of theology; nor even all the principal ones; but those only which appeared to be the most frequently overlooked, or depreciated. That the unbeliever should rank Christianity along with the various systems of superstition which human fraud and folly have produced and maintained, keeping out of sight every circumstance that forms a distinction between the true coin and the counterfeit, is not to be wondered at; but to oppose decided infidelity (though it is hoped some of the arguments adduced may be employed with effect for that purpose) has not been made the primary object of these Essays. I have had in view the case of those who regard Christianity with *indifference*, rather than of those who reject it.

It is a more common, and not a less pernicious, error, to regard Christianity as little else than the religion of nature, proclaimed by a special mission, for the benefit, chiefly, of those whose feebleness of intellect, ignorance, or depraved disposi-

tion, unfits them for discovering its truths
by the light of Reason.   The Gospel accordingly, while praised as a beautiful system, and highly extolled for its utility, is
praised, in fact, for what does not belong
to it, viz. its containing nothing of importance which a philosophical mind might not
discover by its own unaided powers: and
is regarded as useful only for the less
intelligent, and less cultivated; in short,
for the vulgar.

There are others, again, whose venera-
tion for the Gospel is more real, but who
erroneously think to honour and support
it by laying a foundation which, in fact,
tends to weaken and degrade the superstructure.   Beginning with natural religion, they attribute to that much of what
properly belongs to Christianity, and much
that belongs to neither; and thus often
lead to the perversion of some parts of the
Gospel, and to the depreciation of others.
In fact, the study of natural religion ought

properly to *follow*, or at least to accompany, not to precede, that of revelation. Our own speculations ought to be controlled and regulated by a divine revelation, when it is once ascertained that a revelation exists: they should not be left to range unlimited and unassisted, on a subject on which God has Himself decided that man is not competent of himself to judge rightly. And if Reason be for some time enthroned as sole judge and lawgiver, she will not afterwards readily resign her seat, and submit her decisions, to Revelation; but will often exercise an undue interference. It is sometimes complained, that the mind is unduly biassed in its judgments by continual reference to the authority of the Scriptures; and the complaint is just, if the Scriptures are *not* the word of God: if they are, there is an opposite and corresponding danger to be guarded against; that of suffering the mind to be unduly biassed in the study and interpretation of the revealed will of God, by the deductions of unaided reason.

Respecting the peculiarities about to be noticed, various misconceptions are afloat, according to the diversity both of the several points in question, and of the habits of mind of different individuals: a circumstance may be either utterly overlooked and disregarded;—or it may be supposed not connected with, or not peculiar to, our religion, while in fact it is so;—or its importance may be under-rated. This variety in the errors to be guarded against, must give rise occasionally to a corresponding variety in the topics dwelt on; and the necessity of thus shifting the attention successively to different quarters, may, it is feared, give a desultory and interrupted appearance to some parts of the work: but the inconvenience is one which cannot be entirely avoided, when it is necessary, within a moderate compass, to maintain and illustrate, with a view to different descriptions

of readers, several different positions, all
intimately connected with the main object.

Numerous, indeed, and various are the
misapprehensions which have prevailed
(not to advert to heresies which have been
formally stigmatized as such) respecting
the peculiarities of the Christian religion:
for as on the one hand many deny to
the Gospel much of what belongs to it,
or refer to the religion of nature, much
that belongs *exclusively* to Christianity,
so, on the other hand, many, and sometimes even the same, persons attribute to
the Gospel revelation what forms no part
of it; or represent that as peculiar to it,
which really does lie within the reach of
natural reason. A familiar instance of
this last is the representation given by
some of the doctrine of the corrupt nature
of man; which they represent as a truth
resting on revelation, and claiming to be
acknowledged as an article of faith not
discoverable by reason: whereas daily ex-

perience sufficiently proves it; and though there are still, and ever will be, some who will not learn from experience, men of sense, in all ages, seem to have fallen little, if at all, short of the truth, in that point. The *history* indeed of the fall of man is revealed in Scripture; but the actual *condition* of man, though often adverted to, can hardly be said to be *revealed* in Scripture, any more than the truths, that the sun shines by day and the moon by night. The origin of evil, again, not a few are apt to speak of, as explained and accounted for, at least in great part, by the Scripture accounts of " sin entering into the world, and death by sin;" whereas the Scriptures leave us, with respect to the difficulty in question, just where they find us, and are manifestly not designed to remove it. He who professes to *account* for the existence of evil, by merely tracing it up to the *first* evil recorded as occurring, would have no reason to deride the absurdity of an atheist, who should profess to account for the origin of the human race, without having recourse to a Creator, by simply tracing them up to the *first* pair.

Errors of this class, however, the nature of my design, in the following Essays, will only allow me to notice slightly and incidentally: the principal object proposed being to guard against those of the opposite description; which tend to the depreciation, and ultimately the neglect, of Christianity, by keeping out of sight, or under-rating, many of its great and important peculiarities.

Bishop Warburton's "Divine Legation" is a work too well known to require that a distinct reference should be made to it in every place in which I have availed myself of his learning and ingenuity. I can hardly be suspected of wishing to impose on the public as my own, what I have borrowed from an author who has so long been before them. To have exhibited clearly

in a small space, separated from extraneous
matter, and from topics of temporary con-
troversy, some of the most important parts
of an inestimably valuable, but voluminous,
digressive, and incomplete work, may
prove advantageous not only to such as
have not studied the work, but, in some
degree, to many also even of those who are
familiar with it.

ESSAY I.

ON A FUTURE STATE.

THE doctrine of man's immortality, when once the mind can be brought to dwell intently on the subject, is certainly the most interesting and the most important that can be presented to him. Other objects may, and often do, occupy more of our attention, and take a stronger hold of our feelings; but that in real importance, all those objects are comparatively trifles, no one can doubt. Other matters of contemplation, again, may be, in themselves, not less awful, stupendous, and wonderful; but none of these can so intimately concern ourselves. Admirable as is the whole of God's creation, no other of his works can be so interesting to man, as man himself; sublime as is the idea of the eternal Creator himself, our *own* eternal existence after death is an idea calculated to strike *us* with still more overpowering emotions. That man, feeble and shortlived as he appears on earth, is destined by his Maker to live for ever—that ages hence, when we and our remotest posterity shall have been long forgotten on earth—and countless ages yet beyond, when this earth itself, and perhaps a long succession of other worlds, shall have come to an end—we shall still be living; still sensible of pleasure or pain, to a greater degree perhaps than our present nature admits of, and still having no shorter space of existence before us than at first—these are thoughts which overwhelm the imagination the more, the longer it dwells upon them. The understanding cannot adequately embrace the truths it is compelled to acknowledge: and when, after intently gazing for some time on this vast prospect, we turn aside to contemplate the various courses of earthly events and transactions, which seem like rivulets trickling into the boundless ocean of eternity, we are struck with a sense of the infinite insignificance of all the objects around us that have a reference to our present state alone; while every the most minute circumstance, that may concern the future life, like a seed from which some mighty tree is to spring, rises into immeasurable importance, as the awful reflection occurs that perhaps something which is taking place at this very moment may contribute to fix our final destiny. There is no one truth, in short, the conviction of which tends to produce so total a change in our estimate of all things.

The powerful influence which such a belief is likely to have on the conduct of those who keep it habitually before them, is too obvious to need being insisted on: but it may be interesting, and not unprofitable, to enquire, by *whom* a doctrine thus sublime in contemplation, thus important in practice, was first proposed to us; by whom "life and immortality were brought to light:" proposed, I mean, not as a matter of curious speculation, and interesting conjecture, but as a point of general, and well-grounded, and practical belief; brought to light, not as an ingenious and pleasing theory, but as an established truth; displayed to us, not as a wandering meteor that serves but to astonish and amuse us, but as the great luminary which is destined to brighten our prospect, and to direct our steps.

Now that "Jesus Christ brought life and immortality to light through the Gospel," and that, in the most literal sense, which implies that the revelation of this doctrine is *peculiar* to his Gospel, seems to be at least the most obvious meaning of the Scriptures of the New Testament. The doctrine in question, which occupies a very prominent place in the preaching of the Apostles, appears in general to be taught by them not as one already well established, resting on sufficient evidence, and which they had only to acknowledge and confirm, but as a part of the *revelation* which they were commissioned to communicate.

That infidels who admit the doctrine should reject this account of its establishment, is at least consistent; but there are not a few among Christians who seem to regard it as a truth, not only discoverable, but actually discovered, by unassisted human reason; and who have maintained, that though debased and perverted in form by ignorant superstition, it has been in substance fully and generally admitted, in almost all ages and countries. And there have been others, who, though not going the length of making this knowledge a part of *natural* religion, and ascribing it to the *Pagan* nations of antiquity, have yet insisted that it is a part of the revelation given through Moses to the Israelites.

In favour of the first of these opinions, it is often pleaded, in addition to the direct arguments drawn from the Pagan writers, that to deny the power of reason to establish this truth, is to weaken the foundation of natural religion, and to diminish the support it affords to Christianity: it is even contended by one writer of no small repute, that " the natural revolutions and resurrections of other creatures render the resurrection of the body highly probable. The day dies into a night, and is buried in silence and in darkness; in the next morning it appeareth again and reviveth, opening the grave of darkness, rising from the dead of night; this is a diurnal resurrection. As the day dies into night, so doth the summer into winter;" &c. &c. &c. In favour of the latter also of the above-mentioned opinions it has been urged, that to acknowledge no revelation of a future state in the law of Moses is "derogatory to God's honour, injurious to the Mosaic dispensation, a very erroneous and dangerous doctrine," &c. &c. and this in a discourse on the very text which asserts that "Jesus Christ brought life and immortality to light through the Gospel!" To reconcile this passage with such opinions, (which a Christian who entertains them is evidently bound to do,) has been attempted in a manner which may fairly be designated *explaining away* those words of the Apostle; and indeed not those words only, but the general tenor of the whole of the preaching of the Apostles, as far as relates to the point in question; so as to lay them open to the censure of giving an overcharged representation of the Gospel scheme, when they characterize it as " bringing life and immortality to light."

I shall not, however, at present dwell on this inconsistency, because as long as the notion remains unrefuted, that the doctrine of a future immortality could be known, and was known, independently of the Gospel, to prove that the first preachers of Christianity professed to exhibit the first revelation of that truth, would be only to expose them to the imputation of groundless pretensions, and thus to give a colour to the cavils of the infidel, who is ready enough to charge them with falsely laying claim to the original announcement of a doctrine already well established.

It will be advisable therefore to enquire first into the notions entertained on this subject by the ancient Pagans and by the Jews, and the grounds on which those notions rested; in order that the questions may be, as far as possible, decided, how far natural reason, and how far the Mosaic revelation, are calculated, in this respect, to supersede the Gospel, in affording a rational and a well-established assurance of a future state. I say, " well-established," because if the doctrine were made to rest on the most decisive evidence, but on such evidence as could not be comprehended by any but profound philosophers, the mass of mankind would still need a revelation to assure them of it. On the other hand, I say " rational" as well as " established," because however general and *confident* the belief of it might be, if that belief rested on no "rational" grounds, it would still need to be made known (since conjecture is not knowledge) on sufficient authority. It is important therefore to remember, that there are two points, neither of which should be lost sight of in the present enquiry: in what degree the belief of a future state *prevailed* among the ancients; and how far those who did entertain such belief were *correct* in their notions of it, and *warranted* in maintaining them: since it is plain, that no opinion deserves to be called knowledge, except so far as it is not only agreeable to truth, but also supported by adequate evidence.

The popular mythology of the Greeks and Romans (to direct our attention in the first place to the Pagan nations) did certainly contain ample descriptions of a life after this, and of the places prepared for the reward and punishment, respectively, of the virtuous and the wicked. And though it might be urged, with truth, that this mythology, resting as it did on no other evidence than that of vague, and incoherent, and contradictory tradition, could not afford any *rational* assurance of a future state [a], and also that it did not inculcate the doctrine of a *resurrection*, and was in many other points greatly at variance with what Christians receive as the authentic and true account; still it must be admitted, that a system so far correct in its outline as to contain the notion of a just judgment, and a state of retribution hereafter, to be influenced by our conduct during the present life, would, in some degree, supply the want of the Gospel revelation on these points; provided it were (on whatever evidence) fully and firmly and generally *established* among the mass of the com-

---

[a] Such, of course, must be the case with the notions of Pagans of the present day on the subject, as well as with those of the barbarous nations of antiquity, of whose mythology we have no distinct and authentic accounts. How far the doctrine of a future state did or does prevail, and prevail as a matter of *serious belief*, in those nations, it is by no means easy to determine on sufficient evidence. In those of modern times it is also difficult, if not impossible, to decide, whether, and to what degree, some parts of their religion may have been derived, through a remote and corrupt tradition, from the Gospel. The fairest mode of trying the question therefore seems to be, by examining the opinions that prevailed *before* the promulgation of the Gospel.

munity. Now that this was not the case, with respect to the accounts of a future state current among the ancients, is the conclusion which will present itself to any one who examines the question fully and candidly: I say, fully and candidly, because one whose researches are very limited, will not be unlikely to have met with such passages only in ancient writers as would, of themselves, lead to a contrary conclusion; and one who is strongly prepossessed in favour of that conclusion, will confine his attention to those passages, seeking only to explain away all that militate against it. The truth is, there *are* many passages to be found (and that, frequently in the same authors) of each description; some that seem to imply the general belief, and others the disbelief, of the accounts of a future life. But it should be remembered, that, in such a case, the latter are entitled to the greater weight: for there can be no doubt that the fables of Elysium and Tartarus were a part of the popular religion, which it was usually thought decorous to speak of with respect; and the doctrine of a future state was regarded as especially expedient to be inculcated on the vulgar, in order to restrain them in cases beyond the control of human laws ; so that a good reason can be assigned for a philosopher's appearing to consider the doctrine as indubitable, though he neither believed it himself, nor could flatter himself that it was so generally believed as he might think desirable : whereas on the other hand no reason whatever can be assigned for any one's treating it as a fable, if he really did believe it. When then we find Socrates and his disciples represented by Plato as fully admitting in their discussion of the subject, that " men in general were highly incredulous as to the soul's future existence," and as expecting that " it would, at the moment of our natural death, be dispersed (as he expresses it) like air or smoke, and cease altogether to exist, so that it would require no little persuasion and argument to convince them that the soul can exist after death, and can retain any thing of its powers and intelligence ;"—when we find this, I say, asserted, or rather alluded to, as notoriously the state of popular opinion, we can surely entertain but little doubt that the accounts of

Elysium and Tartarus were regarded as mere poetical fables, calculated to amuse the imagination, but unworthy of serious belief.

It may be thought, however, (though the supposition does not seem a probable one,) that the philosopher mistook, or misrepresented, the opinions of his countrymen: let us turn to the records of matters of fact, as presented to us by an able and faithful historian, who possessed the amplest opportunities for obtaining information. The testimony of Thucydides, not as to the *professed* belief, but as to the conduct, of the Athenians, under those trying circumstances in which the near approach of death impresses the most forcibly the thought of a future state on the minds of those who expect it—his testimony, I say, as to their conduct on such an occasion, must alone prove almost decisive of the question. For it will hardly be denied, that those who firmly believe in a future state, or even regard it as a thing highly probable, however the pursuits and occupations of this world may have drawn off their attention from it, will be likely, when death evidently draws near—death, not in the tumultuous ardour of battle, but in the calm, yet resistless, progress of disease—to think with lively and anxious interest of the life of another world. If they have any apprehensions at all of judgment to come, they will usually wish to " die the death of the righteous," even though they may not have been willing to lead the life of the righteous. Even those who have been in some doubt respecting this truth, or who have studied to keep it out of sight, are generally found to believe in it the most firmly at that awful moment, when they would be most glad to disbelieve it; and then to think most of it, when the thought is the most intolerable.

It is not necessary for the present purpose to contend, that what has been just said constitutes a rule without exception; let it be admitted only as applying to the generality, or even to a considerable portion merely, of mankind; (and thus far at least we are surely borne out, both by reason and experience;) and let any one with these principles before him contemplate the picture drawn of the pestilence which ravaged Athens during the Peloponnesian war, by that judicious historian who was an eye-witness and a partaker of the calamity. Whether the ancient poets, or philosophers, be regarded as the better instructors in the doctrine of a future state, Athens had no deficiency in either: and a plague so wide-spreading, so irresistible, and which brought with it to those whom it seized (as we are expressly told) such an utter despair of recovery, may be fairly expected to have had the effect, in some minds at least, of awakening whatever belief, or even suspicion, they might have entertained respecting Tartarus and Elysium, and of calling into action their fears and hopes on the subject. We might expect to find *some* of them at least bewailing their sins, making reparation to those they had injured, and in every way striving to prepare for the judgment that seemed impending.

The very reverse took place. The historian tells us, that " seeing death so near them, they resolved to make the most of life while it lasted, by setting at nought all laws divine and human, and eagerly plunging into every species of profligacy." Nor was this conduct by any means confined to the most vile and worthless of the community; for he complains of a general and permanent *depravation* of morals, which dated its origin from this calamity. Nor again does the description apply to such only as had been, either openly or secretly, contemners of the whole system of the national religion; for we are told, that "at first many had recourse to the offices of their religion, with a view to appease the gods; but that when they found their sacrifices and ceremonies *availed nothing against the disease*, and that the pious and the impious alike fell victims to it, they at once concluded that piety and impiety were altogether indifferent, and cast off all religious and moral obligations." Is it not evident from this, that those who did reverence the gods, had been accustomed to look for none but *temporal* rewards and punishments from them? Can we conceive that men who expected that virtue should be rewarded, and vice punished, in the other world, would, just at their entrance into that world, *begin* to regard virtue and vice as indifferent?

It is but too true, indeed, that men have been found, in countries where Christianity is professed, so hardened, as to manifest, even at the approach of death, no regard to the judgment which is to succeed it; who have availed themselves of present impunity for the commission of crimes, or have endeavoured to drown thought in sensual excess: but instances of this kind rather go to prove that such men do *not*, than that the heathens *did*, believe in a future retribution; if by belief is to be understood, not a mere unthinking assent, or a mere *non-denial*, of the doctrine, but a deliberate, firm, and habitual conviction. Such gross and complete ignorance is to be found in not a few of the lower orders in professedly Christian countries, that scarcely any idea whatever of religion has at any time entered their minds. If this assertion should appear, as it probably may, to some of my readers overcharged, or if they should suppose that instances of this kind must be, in this country at least, extremely rare, they may convince themselves but too easily of the deplorable truth, either by enquiring of those, who in the discharge of their clerical functions have had opportunity to ascertain it, or by themselves examining such of the least educated among the lower orders (and many, I fear I may add, much above the lowest) who come in their way; among whom they will, I am convinced, meet with instances of persons growing up to maturity with scarcely any more knowledge or thought concerning the Christian religion, than the Hindoo mythology. Those again who have been long hardened in habits of extreme profligacy, may ultimately become as blind to all ideas of a future state as if they had never heard of it: but experience as well as reason forbids us to believe, that, where the Gospel is assiduously preached, such a degree of ignorance, or of depravity, can ever be general, much less universal. And, accordingly, it appears, that the great plague which desolated London, produced, on the whole, an effect exactly opposite to that at Athens. Some abandoned wretches, no doubt, took the same advantage as the Athenians did, of the calamity; but the generality seem plainly to have shewn, that their belief of a future state, however it might have lain dormant during a time of apparent security, and however easily it might be thrown off on a return to such a state, was real and deep-rooted. No instances are recorded *there* of pious men *renouncing* their piety when they saw death approaching : on the contrary, serious devotion seems for the most part to have prevailed, and, if not reformation, at least alarm and contrition, to have been generally produced among sinners. Many are said, when attacked by the plague, to have even rushed into the public streets, confessing aloud and bewailing crimes long ago committed, and never before imputed to them, and earnestly seeking to make reparation. Now it may surely be presumed, that instances of this kind, if they occurred at all, at Athens, must have been rare indeed ; that no one such took place is the most probable inference ; since none are recorded. The account indeed which the historian gives of the general depravity that supervened, is certainly not to be understood without exceptions ; for he tells us, that *some good* men retained their virtue, and displayed their humanity ; but had any instances occurred of the *repentance* of *bad* men—of sinners alarmed into remorse for their guilt, and endeavouring to atone for it—such instances would have presented so striking a contrast to the general case, that we can hardly suppose a writer so accurate and intelligent, living on the spot, would have made no mention of them.

In Christian countries, on the contrary, however *imperfectly* Christian, in respect of many of the inhabitants of them, it is well known that instances of this kind are of daily occurrence, even when the ordinary course of human mortality is not accelerated by any remarkable visitation.

Can we then, on comparing two such cases together, come to the conclusion, that in each, the notions respecting a future state were the same, or at all similar? Is not the obvious inference, that, at least the Athenians of that age, considered the accounts of a future life as no more than amusing fictions, of whose utter falsity there was no reason even to doubt?

And that the prevailing belief at other times, and in other states, Greek or Italian, was the same as at Athens at the period just spoken of, there is at least a strong presumption, till evidence of the contrary is produced. The Athenians were noted for their religious devotion; the popular mythology which prevailed among the other Grecian states, and, I may add, at Rome, was the same, or nearly the same, with theirs; and therefore may be presumed, in the absence of all proof to the contrary, to have had the same results in respect of the belief of a future life: which therefore, though nominally professed, cannot be considered as practically forming any part of the creed of those ancient nations with whom we are best acquainted. When at Athens St. Paul came to speak of the resurrection of the dead, some of his hearers mocked; and when Festus heard of the resurrection from the dead, he exclaimed, " Paul, thou art beside thyself." So far indeed were the promulgators of Christianity from finding the belief of a future state already well established, that they appear to have had no small difficulty in convincing of this truth even some of their converts. Some of those who denied a *resurrection*, may indeed with good reason be supposed to have looked for some other kind of future existence; but when St. Paul finds it necessary to urge, " if *in this life only we have hope* in Christ, we are of all men most miserable—let us eat and drink, for to-morrow we die," it is plain that he must have been opposing such as expected *nothing* beyond the grave.

It may be said, however, (and this perhaps is the most prevailing notion,) that little as the vulgar believed in the doctrine of a future state, it was received and inculcated by many eminent philosophers. Now that a truth of the highest importance to all mankind alike should be discovered by a few, and confined to them, would be, even if the fact were fully established, no very great triumph of human reason. But, in reality, the doctrine never was either generally admitted among the ancient philosophers, or satisfactorily proved by any of them, even in the opinion of those who argued in favour of it. On the one hand, not only the Epicurean school openly contended against it, but one of much greater weight than any of them, and the founder of a far more illustrious sect, Aristotle, without expressly combating the notion of a future state, does much more; he passes it by as not worth considering, and takes for granted the contrary supposition, as not needing proof. He remarks incidentally, in his treatise on courage, that " death is formidable beyond most other evils, on account of its excluding hope; since it is a complete termination, and there does not appear to be *any thing either of good or evil* beyond it[b]." And in the same work, in discussing the question whether a man can justly be pronounced happy before the end of his life, he proceeds all along (as indeed is the case throughout) on the supposition, that after death a man ceases altogether to exist[c]. And it should be observed, that his incidental and oblique allusion to this latter opinion, implies (as I have said) much more than if he had expressly asserted and maintained it; in *that* case he would have borne testimony only to his *own* belief; but as it is, we may collect from his mode of speaking that such was the *prevailing*, and generally uncontradicted, belief of the rest of the world.

[b] Arist. Eth. Nicom. b. iii.   [c] Ibid. b. i.

Of those philosophers again, who contended
for a future state, it is to be observed, not only
that, as Dr. Paley remarks, they did not, properly speaking, effect a *discovery;* "it was
only one guess among many; he only dis-
covers, who proves;" but also, that (as has
been said above) their arguments did not fully
succeed in convincing even themselves. Those
which at one time they bring forward as decisive proof, they seem at another time to regard
as hardly possessing that degree of probability,
which, now that the doctrine is established,
most are ready to allow to them. Cicero
especially, who is frequently appealed to on
this question, we find distinctly acknowledging, at least in the person of one of his dis-
putants, that though, while he is reading the
Phædo, he feels disposed to assent to the
reasons urged in favour of a future state, his
conviction vanishes as soon as he lays down
the book, and resolves the matter in his own
thoughts: which was the feeling probably
with which the author himself had written it [d].

[d] Not that this inconsistency in their writings implies a
corresponding hesitation and vacillation in their opinions; but

Many indeed of the deistical writers of modern times have come to much more decisive conclusions, on this, and also on many other points, than the ancients did, and indeed than are fairly warranted by any arguments which unassisted reason can supply: but this only affords a presumption of the powerful, though unacknowledged and perhaps unperceived, influence which the Gospel revelation has exercised even on the minds of those who reject it: they have drunk at that stream of knowledge, which they cannot, or will not, trace to the real source from which it flows.

Supposing however those of the ancient philosophers, who maintained a future state, to have been more fully convinced themselves of the conclusions they respectively arrived at, than it appears they really were, it is evidently necessary to enquire in the next place, what those conclusions were, and on what proofs

evidently because most of them, except the Epicureans, judged it necessary to keep the vulgar in awe, by the terrors of another world; which accordingly they very gravely set forth and insist on in their popular (exoteric) works. See note (A) at the end of this Essay.

they rested. The arguments commonly employed by them, (and also by such deists of the present day as admit the doctrine,) viz. the distinct nature of the soul from the corruptible body with which it is united—the vigour and energy which the soul sometimes manifests when the body is in the lowest state of exhaustion, &c. led them naturally to the inference, that the soul will continue to exist after death in a *separate* state, never to be re-united with matter. They represented the body as a kind of prison of the spiritual part, from which it was to be released by death; and the soul accordingly would energize, they supposed, more freely, and enjoy the happiness of more exalted contemplation, when freed from its connexion with gross material substance.

To this it was replied, that the body seems rather the necessary organ of the soul, than its prison; that the effects frequently produced by external injuries, by the administration of certain drugs, and by several, though not all, bodily diseases, sufficiently shew the dependence of the mental functions on the body; and that the perceptive powers of the mind, which are the main source of our knowledge, must apparently lie dormant, without the intervention of the bodily senses[e]: "how," said they, "can the soul enjoy, when the eye and the ear, for instance, are destroyed, those perceptions which are furnished by sight and hearing?" The whole argument is detailed in Lucretius with considerable ingenuity; and though he goes much too far, in thence concluding that the soul *cannot possibly* exist in an active and perceptive state without the body—much more, when he contends that it cannot exist at all, (for how can we tell that *other* means of perception, such as we have no

[e] Some writers are accustomed to adduce instances of great mental energy remaining in the midst of bodily decay, unimpaired even up to the moment of dissolution, as a proof of the mind's independence on the body; but surely this is a very incorrect way of reasoning, especially when the cases brought forward are manifestly exceptions to the general rule. To prove that the mental faculties are not dependent on *every* part of the bodily organization, does not authorize us to conclude that they are connected with *no* part of it: a disease may attack a vital part of the bodily system, and yet leave unhurt to the last those parts (supposing there are such) which are connected with the exercise of the mental powers.

notion of, may not be substituted ?)—still it must be admitted, that he leaves the question in a doubtful state, and reduces the opposite conclusion to no more, at the utmost, than a faint probability. At least, nothing more can be fairly claimed for it, till some more satisfactory answer (drawn from reason, independent of revelation) can be given to the above objections, than any that has hitherto appeared[f].

[f] A well known argument by illustration, which has been employed on this subject, will be found on examination to be less solid than ingenious. If we suppose, it has been said, a person to have been kept from his birth in a dark cave, which admits a portion of light, and a partial view of external objects, only through an aperture in the wall that closes its entrance, would he not, thus accustomed to receive all his perceptions through that aperture, suppose, that this loop-hole is essential to them, and that if it were destroyed, he should be left in total obscurity? yet we know, that if the wall were pulled down, and the whole cave thrown open, he would enjoy a fuller light and a much wider prospect. Even so we, it is urged, who are accustomed to receive all our perceptions through the medium of the bodily senses, are apt to suppose, though with no better reason, that the destruction of the body would leave us without the means of perception; whereas, in fact, the soul might then be released, as it were, from a cave, and enjoy a wider sphere of intelligence and of activity. There is a speciousness in this illustration very likely to captivate

To the Christian, indeed, all this doubt would be instantly removed, if he found that the immortality of the soul, as a disembodied spirit, were revealed to him in the word of God: he cannot question the power of the great Creator to prolong, in any way he may

a superficial enquirer; but in fact, if it proves any thing at all, it militates against the conclusion drawn from it. The fallacy consists in overlooking, (what is commonly overlooked in many similar cases, into which much error and confusion of thought are thus introduced,) that an *aperture* is a *negative* idea, implying merely the *absence* of a certain portion of opaque matter. The supposed person in the cave, therefore, would not in reality be at all mistaken in his notions and expectations; for he supposes, not that the opaque substance of the sides of the cave is necessary to his perceptions, but, on the contrary, that the *interruption* or absence of that opaque body is so; in which he would be perfectly right: as he would also in supposing that the destruction of that aperture would put an end to his perception; since that destruction would be properly the *closing* of the aperture, not the throwing down of the walls, which would in truth be an *enlargement* of it. Now the body and the bodily senses being evidently not merely negative ideas, the destruction of them bears no analogy whatever to the supposed destruction of the cave; since that cave itself was never imagined to be, to the person enclosed, (as the bodily senses are to us,) the means of conveying knowledge, but, on the contrary, as far as it extends, of excluding it.

see fit, the life he originally gave: but this is very different from arriving at the conclusion by the evidence which unassisted reason can supply. In fact, however, no such doctrine *is* revealed to us; the Christian's hope, as founded on the promises contained in the Gospel, is, the resurrection of the *body*[g]; a doctrine which seems never to have occurred (nor indeed was likely to occur, from any contemplation of the change from night to day, and from summer to winter) to any of the heathen. Indeed, when any of them are struck by, and notice, any phenomenon in nature that has the appearance of a *revival*, they are struck by it as a *contrast* to the supposed fate of man. Thus we find a Greek poet, in bewailing a departed friend, lamenting, that while the herbs of the garden, which appear dead, shoot up in the succeeding spring, man, on the contrary, who appears a being of so much greater dignity, when dead, is doomed to live no more:

Ὁππότε πρᾶτα θάνωμες, ἀνάκοσι ἐν χθονὶ κοίλᾳ
Εὕδομες εὖ μάλα μακρὸν, ΑΤΕΡΜΟΝΑ, ΝΗΓΡΕΤΟΝ
ὕπνον.

[g] See note (B) at the end of this Essay.

As, however, even the faintest conjecture of a
future existence, though it must not be confounded with a full assurance of it, is, as far as
it goes, an approximation towards the knowledge of truth, so, also, notions considerably
incorrect respecting that existence, if they are
but such as to involve the idea of enjoyment
or suffering, corresponding with men's conduct
in this life, have so far something of a just
foundation, and of a tendency to practical
utility. This, however, appears by no means
to have been the case with the systems of any,
as far as we can learn, of those ancient philosophers, who contended the most strenuously
for the immortality of the soul. For not only
do they seem to have agreed, that no suffering
could be expected by the wicked in another
life, on the ground that the gods were incapable of anger, and therefore could not punish;
but the very notion of the soul's immortality,
as explained by them, involved the complete
destruction of distinct personal existence.
Their notion was, (I mean, when they spoke
their real sentiments; for in their *exoteric* or
popular works they often inculcate, for the

benefit of the vulgar, the doctrine of future retribution, which they elsewhere laugh at,) that the soul of each man is a portion of that spirit which pervades the universe [h], to which it is re-united at death, and becomes again an undis-tinguishable part of the great whole; just as the body is resolved into the general mass of matter [i]. So that their immortality, or rather eternity of the soul, was anterior as well as posterior; as it was to have no end, so it had no beginning; and the boasted continuance of existence, which according to this system we are to expect after death, consists in returning to the state in which we were before birth; which, every one must perceive, is the same thing, virtually, with annihilation.

Let it be remembered then, when the argu-ments of the heathen sages are triumphantly brought forward in proof of the soul's immor-tality, that when they countenanced the doc-

---

[h] See note (C) at the end of this Essay.

[i] " Whatever there is," says Cicero, (*Fragm. de Conso-latione,*) " that perceives, that exercises judgment, that wills, is of celestial nature, and divine; and for that reason it must of necessity be eternal."

trine of future retribution, they taught, with a view to political expediency, what they did not themselves believe ; and that when they spoke their real sentiments on the subject, the eternity of existence which they expected, as it implied the destruction of all distinct personality, amounted practically to nothing at all.

It is not unlikely, that in thus depreciating the power of unassisted reason to ascertain the truth of a future life, I shall be suspected of favouring some opinions against which much clamour has been raised, viz. that the soul is naturally mortal—incapable of an existence continued after our dissolution, except from the express decree of the Creator; and that it is a material substance, or an attribute of matter.

It were to be wished, that those who have agitated these questions (and indeed many others) had begun by distinctly ascertaining what they were disputing about; which neither of the parties appear to have attended to. For my own part, I must frankly acknowledge, that I do not understand the questions. If by " nature " is meant the course in which the

Author and Governor of all things proceeds in his works, (which is the only meaning I am able to attach to it,) then, to say that the souls of men, if God has appointed that they shall exist for ever, are naturally immortal, is not only an undeniable but an identical proposition; it is only saying that the appointments of Omnipotence will surely take effect. If on the other hand, when it is said that the soul is naturally mortal, nothing more is meant than that its existence is maintained after death solely by the agency of divine power; this also I should not only fully admit, but should extend to our present existence also; "for in God we live, and move, and have our being :" I cannot conceive what are called *physical causes* to possess power, in the strict sense of the word [k]; or

---

[k] It is a remarkable circumstance, that both in the Greek and Latin languages, nouns of the neuter gender, *i. e.* considered as denoting *things*, and not *persons*, (for though many really inanimate objects were expressed by masculine and feminine nouns, it is evident they were personified, by the very circumstance of sex being attributed to them,) invariably had the nominative and accusative the same; or rather, may be said to have had an accusative only, employed as a nominative when the grammatical construction required it; for the nomi-

to be capable of maintaining, more than of first producing, the system of the universe; whose continued existence, no less than its origin, seems to me to depend on the continual operation of the great Creator. The laws of nature, as they are called, presuppose (as Dr. Paley remarks) an agent; since they are "the modes in which that agent operates;" they cannot be the cause of their own observance.

The principles here touched upon (which it would be foreign to the present purpose to

native, so called, of neuter nouns, corresponds to the *accusative* (if to any case) of masculines; *e. g.* the accusative of " dominus" is " dominum;" and accordingly, under the same declension we have " regn-*um*," both nominative and accusative. A rule of this kind extending without exception to several declensions, and both numbers, in two languages, can hardly be a mere accident. May it not have arisen from an indistinct consciousness that a *person* only can really be an *agent;* a mere thing, being, in truth, only *acted upon?* And may not the same cause have led to the practice in Greek, of joining a neuter plural with a verb in the singular?

I throw out this suggestion with a full expectation that by many it will be derided as fanciful; but they cannot deny that the *phenomenon exists*, and must have *some* cause; and the fairest and most decisive objection to any proposed solution of it is, *to offer a better.*

explain and defend) may, I am aware, be disputed by many who are far from having any leaning towards atheism; but that they are at all of a mischievous tendency, even if erroneous, can hardly be contended by any one of the smallest degree of candour.

The question again respecting the materiality of the soul, is one which I am also at a loss to understand clearly, till it shall have been clearly determined *what matter is.* We know nothing of it, any more than of mind, except its attributes; and, let it not be forgotten, the most remarkable of these are not ascertained. Whether Gravitation be an essential quality of matter is still a question, and likely to remain so, among natural philosophers; who accordingly are divided in opinion whether those commonly called *imponderable* substances, Heat, Light, and Electricity, are Substances at all, or not. At any rate, let not the truths of religion be rested on any decision respecting subtle questions which belong to the natural philosopher or the metaphysician, not the theologian; nor let our hopes in God's promises be mixed up with debates about extension, and gravitation, and form. The Scriptures in these points leave us just where they found us; giving no explanation of the nature of the soul, but giving us instead, what is far more important, an assurance that we are destined to live for ever. That this is *impossible*, and that no revelation is to be received, however attested, which contains this doctrine, we may be assured no metaphysical arguments will ever prove; and it is on the other hand, I think, equally out of the power of metaphysical arguments to prove the contrary; to establish, without the aid of divine revelation, the *certainty* of a future immortality[1]: for if otherwise, whence is it that the wisest of men, when fairly left to themselves, never did arrive at the conclusion, by any arguments which were satisfactory even to themselves.

---

[1] It should not be forgotten, that none of those who contend for the natural immortality of the soul, on the ground of its distinct nature from the body, its incapability of decomposition, &c. have been able to extricate themselves from one difficulty, viz. that all their arguments apply, with exactly the same force, to prove an immortality not only of brutes, but even of plants.

Let it be observed, however, once more, that the full *assurance* of man's immortality is what is here spoken of; which must be carefully distinguished from probable *conjecture.* It is not denied that arguments have been adduced in favour of this conclusion, which may have been, more or less, convincing to many; some of which are justly regarded as possessing considerable weight; and others have been reckoned such, though perhaps without sufficient grounds. It must not be forgotten, however, that most men are very incompetent judges of the force of any argument which tends to a conclusion of which they are already well assured; and are prone to consider as perfectly clear and decisive, such a train of reasoning as would never have prevailed with themselves, if proposed to them while in a state of doubt. When Columbus had discovered the New World, he found men (according to the well known anecdote told of him) who thought it easy to prove beyond a doubt, *a priori*, that such a country must exist; but they forgot that they had not seen the force of these arguments till the discovery had been made.

Of the arguments just alluded to, that which proceeds on the disorder and irregularity apparent in the present world, and the necessity of a future state of retribution, to vindicate the divine justice, would be indeed most satisfactory, if it involved a solution of the great and perplexing question (intimately connected with it) respecting the origin of Evil: but though it may seem to remove the difficulty one step further off, it does not in any degree explain or lessen it [m]; the expectation that at the day of harvest the tares shall be rooted up and burnt, does not at all explain why they were allowed to be sown among the wheat. That there *are* wicked men, experience teaches us; and that they shall be punished, the Scriptures teach us; nor is there any ground for cavilling at this doctrine, since it involves no *greater* difficulty

---

[m] The Scriptures, it should be observed, leave the question concerning the origin of evil just where they find it : Revelation neither *introduces* the difficulty, as some weak opponents contend, nor clears it up, and accounts for it, as is imagined by some not less weak advocates.

I have entered into a fuller discussion of this point in the Appendix, No. 2, to the last edition of Dr. King's Sermon on Predestination.

than the other, which we cannot but admit; but it does not *explain* the fact; nor are we therefore authorized to infer, *a priori*, independent of revelation, a future state of retribution, from the irregularities prevailing in the present life; since that future state does not account fully for those irregularities.

There is much more weight in the argument, that man, at least civilized and cultivated man, not only is capable of a continued course of improvement, which must be cut short by death, but also has a painful apprehension of this, and a disposition to entertain hopes and fears respecting something after death; and that consequently, on the supposition of no future state, the brutes, who enjoy the present moment without any apprehensions and anxieties about futurity, and who arrive at once at the perfection of their nature, must be much better off than man, and much better fitted for their condition, than we are for ours; since our rational nature thus forms an impediment to our satisfaction. Since, therefore, such a constitution of things would be a manifest exception to the general course of nature, inasmuch as in all other cases each being seems admirably adapted to the kind of existence to which it is destined, the inference drawn is, that the present life is not likely to be the whole of man's existence. This argument, though it can scarcely be considered as decisive, possesses, as has been said, a considerable degree of probability: but it should be observed, that, allowing the utmost force both to this argument and to the one above mentioned, though they lead to the inference of a future *state of existence*, yet they have little if any force in proving a future *immortality*. And it is remarkable, that the northern mythology of our Teutonic ancestors (how far it obtained sincere acceptance, we have no sufficient means of judging) represented the glories enjoyed by the brave in the hall of Odin as of long continuance indeed, but destined to have an end, and to last only

> Till Lok shall burst his seven-fold chain,
> And Night resume her ancient reign;

when the gods themselves, with all the heroes who were the objects of their favour, should be overpowered by their adversaries, and finally annihilated. And the Grecian mythology also represented the happiness of Elysium as of limited duration.

The case of the Jews evidently presents a distinct question, inasmuch as they did possess a divine revelation. The supposition that *they* were acquainted, through that revelation, with the doctrine of a future state, does not militate with the conclusion, that *unassisted reason* is inadequate to the discovery; but it certainly is at variance with the full and literal acceptation of the assertion, that "Jesus Christ brought life and immortality to light through the Gospel." That the Mosaic law did contain the revelation in question, has been maintained, as is well known, by many learned men; and the illustrious author of "The Divine Legation" has been assailed by many of them with much acrimony, for denying that position. It has been contended, that it is "*derogatory to God's honour*, and *injurious to the Mosaic dispensation*, &c. to acknowledge no revelation of a future state in the Law:" and expressions like these may perhaps afford a clue to the origin of the opinion held by those who use them. For it is

probable, that it is the cavils, actual or appre-
hended, of infidels, against so important an
omission in the communication made to God's
favoured people, that have contributed mainly
to suggest a reply which consists in a denial
of the fact of such omission : a defence, unfortunately, which gives a great apparent advantage to the adversary, by enabling him to
cavil, with much better reason, at the very
inadequate manner in which this purpose was
accomplished—at the few, and scanty, and
obscure intimations of the doctrine, which the
Law contains, even admitting every text, which
has ever been adduced on that side of the
question, to be interpreted in the manner most
favourable to it.

And this argument, if duly considered, will
be found of such weight, as to amount in fair-
ness to a decision of the question; to prove,
that is, not, of course, that Moses was an
impostor, but that, on the supposition of his
not being such—in other words, of his being
divinely inspired—he could not have been commissioned to inculcate the doctrine of a future
state.

For let it be considered, in the first place, that as the condition of the departed is *unseen*, and as the rewards and punishments of a future life are not only comparatively *remote*, but also must be conceived as of a nature considerably *different* from any thing we can have experienced; from all these causes, it is found necessary that the most repeated assurances and admonitions should be employed, even towards those who have received the doctrine on the most satisfactory authority. A Christian minister accordingly, in these days, finds that his hearers require to be perpetually reminded of this truth, to which they have long since given their assent; and even that with all the pains he takes to inculcate it, in every different mode, he is still but very partially successful in drawing off men's attention from the things of this world, and fixing it on the " unseen things that are eternal." Much more must this have been the case with the Israelites whom Moses was addressing, who were so dull and gross-minded, so childishly short-sighted and sensual, that even the immediate miraculous presence of God among them, of whose judgments and deliverances they had been eye-witnesses, was insufficient to keep them steady in their allegiance to him. Even the temporal sanctions of the law, the plenty and famine, the victory and defeat, and all the other points of that alternative of worldly prosperity and adversity which was set before them—things in their nature so much more easily comprehended by an unthinking and barbarous people, and so much more suited to their tastes—it was found necessary to detail with the utmost minuteness, and to repeat and remind them of in the most impressive manner, in a vast number of different passages[n]. Is not then the conclusion inevitable, that, if to such a people the doctrine of future retribution had been to be revealed, or any traditional knowledge of it confirmed, we should have found it still more explicitly stated, and still more frequently repeated? And when, instead of any thing like this, we have set before us a few scattered texts, which, it is contended, allude to or imply this doctrine, can it be necessary

[n] See note (D) at the end of this Essay.

even to examine whether they are rightly so interpreted? Surely it is a sufficient reply, to say, that if Moses had intended to inculcate such a doctrine, he would have clearly stated and dwelt on it in almost every page: nor is it easy to conceive, how any man of even ordinary intelligence, and not blinded by devoted attachment to an hypothesis, can attentively peruse the books of the Law, abounding as they do with such copious descriptions of the temporal rewards and punishments (in their own nature so palpable) which sanctioned that Law, and with such earnest admonitions grounded on that sanction, and yet can bring himself seriously to believe, that the doctrine of a state of retribution after death, which it cannot be contended is even mentioned, however slightly, in more than a very few passages, formed a part of the Mosaic revelation. And if any one, from a mistaken zeal to vindicate the honour of God's law against infidels, persists in maintaining that this *was* intended, how will he reply to the cavil they will immediately raise against the glaringly inadequate way of fulfilling such an intention? And thus it is, that when men rashly presume to distort the plain meaning of Scripture, for the sake of defending our religion against unsound objections, they expose it to more powerful ones, which they have left themselves without the means of answering.

An unwise attempt to combat Socinian doctrines also, has probably contributed to produce the same bias in the minds of some, whose abilities and learning would else have led them to judge more fairly of the sense of Scripture. When it is urged against Socinians, that on their hypothesis, which explains away the doctrine of the atonement into a mere figure of speech, the Gospel revelation would seem to be of little or no importance, they usually reply, that it established the belief of future retribution: the ready answer to this appears to be, that this belief was already taught in the Old Testament; an assertion which some of the opponents of Socinianism have accordingly undertaken to establish; in conformity with the too common practice of eagerly catching at any argument which seems to bear against an adversary, without stopping to enquire first whether it is well-founded. And this carelessness about Truth seldom fails to be in the end injurious to its cause. In the present case, for instance, the Socinian may immediately reply, " you have furnished a decisive refutation of the doctrine that eternal life is procured by the sacrifice of Christ, and is offered only through faith in his atonement; since to the Jews, certainly, the efficacious sufferings of the Messiah were not revealed; at least, not so as to be understood by the mass of the people; to whom therefore eternal life must have been held out (if at all, as you contend it was) as the direct reward of obedience: the conclusion therefore is inevitable, that unless what Moses taught was false, your account of the Gospel must be false."

Although, however, it has not been deemed necessary here to examine all the passages in the Books of Moses which have been interpreted as relating to a future state, it will be needful to say a few words respecting that one which is cited by our Lord himself against the Sadducees, in proof of the doctrine: " Now that the dead are raised," says he, " even

Moses sheweth at the bush, when he saith, I am the God of Abraham, and the God of Isaac, and the God of Jacob; he is not the God of the dead, but of the living, for all live unto him;" and, for not having drawn this inference, he charges them with " not knowing the Scriptures:" whence it has very rashly been concluded, that the Scriptures he alluded to were intended to *reveal* this doctrine. But can any man of common sense seriously believe, that such a passage as the one before us (which we may suppose was selected by our Lord as at least one of those most to the purpose) could be sufficient to make known to a rude and unthinking people, such as the Israelites when Moses addressed them, the strange and momentous truth, that " the dead are raised?"— that one of the most important parts of the revelation given them (which it must have been, if it were *any* part of it) could have been left to rest on an oblique and incidental implication, while the far simpler and more obvious doctrine of temporal rewards and punishments, was so plainly and so laboriously inculcated? But, in fact, our Lord's declaration by no means amounts to this : the Sadducees of his time *had heard* of the doctrine ; no matter from what quarter ; and their part evidently was, to examine patiently and candidly whether it were true or not ; and this, especially, by a careful study of the sacred books which they acknowledged, in order to judge whether it were conformable to these, or not.

But a passage, which may be decisive of a certain question, when consulted *with a view to that question*, may be utterly insufficient for the far different purpose of *making known*, in the first instance, the truth which it thus *confirms*. The error of confounding together these two things, gives rise to numberless mistakes in other points besides the one now before us : in fact, it is this very fallacy which has principally misled men throughout, with respect to the general question we are considering, as well as in many other doctrines of our religion°: human reason is considered as sufficiently strong to

° Nam neque tam est acris acies in naturis hominum et ingeniis, ut res tantas quisquam *nisi monstratas*, possit videre ; neque tanta tamen in rebus obscuritas, ut eas non penitus acri vir ingenio cernat, si modo adspexerit. *Cic. de Orat.* l. iii. c. 31.

E

discover the doctrine of a future state, because when the doctrine has been *proposed* to our belief by revelation, it perceives probabilities in favour of it; and the same, with many other doctrines also. And thus it is, that a system of what is called natural religion is dressed up, as it were, with the spoils of revelation; and is made such, as men, when fairly left to themselves, and actually guided by the light of nature alone, never did attain to.

It would be tedious, and, after what has been said, I trust, unnecessary, to cite, as might easily be done, a multitude of passages from the Old Testament, in which a reference to the expectations of a future state would have been apposite and almost inevitable, had the belief of such a doctrine prevailed; or to examine those few texts in the New as well as the Old Testament which have been brought forward to prove that a future state was revealed to the Jews. The sixth book of Warburton's Divine Legation contains a copious and learned discussion of this part of the subject: but no one can enter into such an examination, with any thing like a full and

fair view of the question, who does not clearly
embrace, and steadily keep in mind, the argument already adduced, and on which the conclusion mainly rests; viz. that an unthinking
and uncultivated people, such as the Israelites
whom Moses addressed, must have needed, if
it had been designed to reveal to them a future
state, (or even to confirm and establish such a
doctrine already received,) that it should be
perpetually repeated[p], and inculcated in the
most copious and the clearest manner; that,
consequently, since this is not done, it must be
considered as, at least, highly improbable that
such a revelation to them should have been

[p] All admit that Moses *does* hold out, and dwell upon,
temporal promises and threatenings: but the *frequency* and
earnestness with which he enforces this sanction (and on that
it is that the present argument turns) is often under-rated;
few being accustomed to read the books of the law straight
through; and those who do so, being of course inclined to
pass over slightly, any passage which plainly appears to be
merely a repetition of what had been before said; whereas it
is this very repetition that is the most important for the present purpose. I have accordingly subjoined (note (E) at the
end of this Essay) all these passages; that the reader may be
enabled to estimate the more easily their extraordinary number and copiousness.

intended; and that therefore, in the case of
any doubtful passages, which will admit of,
but do not absolutely require, an interpretation
favourable to the affirmative side, a different
interpretation must be allowed to be, antecedently, more probable.

Why Moses was not commissioned to reveal
this momentous truth, is a question that cannot
fail to occur to one who is pursuing such an
enquiry as the present; and it is a question
which we are not competent completely to
answer, because we cannot presume to explain
why the Gospel, which "brought life and immortality to light," was reserved for that precise period at which it was proclaimed; but,
that enquiry—why a different and more imperfect dispensation was needful to prepare the
way for the Gospel,—being waived, as one surpassing man's knowledge and powers, it is
easy to perceive, that the revelation of the doctrine in the Mosaic law, would have been neither necessary nor proper. It was not necessary, for the purpose of affording a sanction to
the law of Moses, because the Israelites alone,
of all the nations of the world, were under an

extraordinary providence, distributing *temporal* rewards and judgments according to their conduct. The necessary foundation therefore of all religion, "that God is a *rewarder* of them that diligently seek him," did not require, as it must in all other nations, the belief in a future retribution, to remedy all the irregularities of God's ordinary providence, which, among this peculiar people, did not exist. Nor again would it have been proper for Moses, commissioned as he was, to promulgate, not the Gospel, but the Law, to proclaim *that* life and Immortality which the Gospel (as had been, no doubt, revealed to *him*) was destined to "bring to light;" much less, to represent eternal happiness as attainable *otherwise* than through the redemption by Christ, which the Gospel holds out as the only efficacious means of procuring it[q]. On this last point, a few observations will

[q] See note (F) at the end of this Essay. Had eternal life been offered as the reward of obedience to the Law, so that the mission of Christ served only to *relax* the terms of the covenant, in favour of those who transgressed the Law, surely St. Paul's expression would have been, (the very reverse of what he uses,) "For what then serveth the GOSPEL? it was *added because of transgressions.*"

be offered presently; but in the mean time it may be remarked, that the slight hints of this doctrine which the books of the prophets contain,—the faint dawnings, as it were, of a scheme, which was to bring "life and immortality to light,"—and which appear more and more bright as they approached the period of that more perfect revelation, are in perfect consistency with the rule I have supposed Moses to have observed; since it is in proportion as they gave more and more clear notices of the Redeemer to come, and in almost constant conjunction with their descriptions of his mission, that the immortal life, to which he was to open the road and lead the way, is alluded to by the prophets; and also, in proportion as the *extraordinary* and regular administration of divine government in this world, by which the Law had been originally sanctioned, and under which the Jews had hitherto lived, was gradually withdrawn. That it was in these writings, and not in those of Moses, that the Jews must have sought for indications of a future state, is strongly confirmed by the opinion of that excellent and learned divine, Joseph Mede, who declares, that he cannot tell on what Scripture authority the Jewish Church could found their belief in a future state, except the well-known passage in Daniel: (chap. xii. ver. 2.) and even of that it may be observed, that it does not necessarily imply a resurrection of *all* men. Doubtless it did not escape that judicious interpreter of prophecy, that there are in the other prophets many allusions to a future state, which were so understood by the inspired authors themselves; as they are by us *Christian* readers; but it does not follow, that the great mass of the people—any besides the studious and discerning few—would be able clearly to perceive such meaning; especially when a different interpretation of those very passages, applicable to temporal deliverances, might, without destroying their sense, be adopted. Nothing appears to *us* more evident, than the description in Isaiah, for instance, of a *suffering* Messiah; yet we well know, that a prosperous and triumphant temporal prince was generally expected by the Jews; and that the frustration of this hope was the grand stumbling-block of the unbelieving among them.

So also, many passages of the prophets, which convey to Christians, who have enjoyed the Gospel revelation, the intimation of a future state, (at least in their secondary sense,) might very easily be otherwise understood; or, at least, might appear not decisive, to those who lived before Jesus Christ had "*abolished death*, and brought life and immortality to light through the Gospel'."

' In the "Harmony of the Law and the Gospel," by Mr. Lancaster, whose general coincidence with my own views I am happy to observe, the author contends, that " the doctrine of a future state was always entertained by the Israelites, though not expressly declared in the Mosaic law ;"—that the silence of Moses would not eradicate their belief;—and that if they had been ignorant of it, they could not have been said with truth to " have much advantage every way" over the Gentiles; but would have been their inferiors in point of religious knowledge, inasmuch as the doctrine formed a part of " the universal religion of mankind." But surely, even on the supposition (which I do not maintain) that the whole nation of Israel utterly disbelieved a future state, the Gentiles could not be said to have much advantage over them in point of religious *knowledge*, from believing, if they really had believed, what they seem to have but very faintly suspected, the current *fables* (for they were no better) respecting another world; viz. that admission into a place of happiness after death was to be procured by *piety* towards the gods; includ-

There is no doubt, however, that some considerable time before our Lord's advent, the

ing under that term, acts of the foulest impurity, and the most infernal cruelty: by due obedience, for instance, to the divine institutions of Cotytto, the Babylonish Venus, who sentenced every female without exception to become a prostitute for hire; and by human sacrifices at the tomb of the defunct. Let no one forget, that such notions of piety were not confined to barbarous nations: even Aristotle, in his projected republic, in which he wisely prohibits the exhibition of indecent objects to youth, is forced to limit himself to the exclusion of young persons from the *temples of those gods, of whose worship such exhibitions formed a necessary part.* And the anecdote of Cato is well known, who withdrew from the theatre, that his presence might not interrupt the sacred impurities of a religious festival. Truly " every abomination of the Lord which he hateth have those nations done *unto their gods:*" and the expectation of future happiness from such gods and such services, could hardly have been reckoned either as religious *knowledge,* or as an *advantage* in point of faith. On the actual belief, however, of the great mass of the Israelites, we have no means of deciding positively; but if any one should suppose most of them to have thought little or nothing, one way or the other, about what should become of them after death, nor consequently to have either believed or disbelieved, properly speaking, the doctrine in question, his conjecture certainly would not be at variance with the representations Moses gives of the grossness of ideas and puerile short-sightedness of the nation; who, while fed by a daily miracle, and promised the especial favour of the Maker of the belief in a future state did become prevalent (though, as the case of the Sadducees proves,

universe, had their minds set on " the flesh-pots of Egypt, and the fish, and the cucumbers, and the leeks." Christians of these days are not surely *more* gross-minded and unthinking than those Israelites; but every one, at least every minister who is sedulous in his duties, must know, that a large proportion of them require to be incessantly reminded, that this life is not the whole of their existence; though the doctrine be one which *is* " expressly declared" in their religion; and that silence on that subject is quite sufficient, if not to eradicate from their minds all *belief*, at least to put an end to all *thought*, about the matter.

It ought to be observed, that, in order to avoid vagueness and ambiguity in speaking of the knowledge of a future state, or of any thing else, we should steadily keep in mind the precise signification of the word Knowledge; which implies, when strictly employed, three things; viz. Truth, Proof, and Conviction. It is plain, that no one can, properly speaking, be said to *know* any thing that is not *true*, however confident his belief of it may be: but even if to this confident belief truth be added, still there is properly no knowledge, unless there is sufficient proof to *justify* such confidence: one man, e. g. may feel fully satisfied that the moon is inhabited, and another may feel equally certain that it is not; and one of them must have truth on his side; but neither in fact possesses knowledge, because neither can have sufficient proof to offer. Lastly, both truth and proof are insufficient to constitute knowledge in the mind of one to whom that proof is not completely satisfactory: it is true, that the angles of a triangle are equal not *universal*) among the Jews. In the second book of Maccabees, a work of small authority indeed as a history, but affording sufficient evidence of the opinions of the writer and his contemporaries, we find not only unequivocal mention of the doctrine, (though by the way not as an *undisputed* point,) but persons represented as *actuated by the motives* which such a doctrine naturally suggests; which doubtless we should, sometimes at least, have met with also in the historical books of the Old Testament, had the same belief prevailed all along. And our Lord himself alludes to the prevailing opinion of the generality of those whom he addresses : " Search the Scriptures, for in them *ye think* ye have eternal life, and they are they that testify of me :" as much as to say, the very prophets who allude to the doctrine of eternal life, do likewise foretel the coming and describe the character of me, the Bestower of it ; these two parts of their inspired word hang

to two right angles; but though Euclid's demonstration of that truth is complete, no one can be said to *know* that they are so, who is not fully convinced by that demonstration, but remains in a state of hesitation.

together; he who is blind to the one, can found no *rational* hope on the other; since "I am the way, and the truth, and the life," and "he that hath the Son hath life, and he that hath not the Son hath not life." This passage indeed, as well as the others to the same purpose in the New Testament, though they imply the prevalence of this tenet among the Jews, and the general *sincerity* and *strength* of their conviction, do not by any means imply either that this their confident expectation was *well founded* on Scriptural evidence, or that their notions respecting a future life were *correct*. Had these last two circumstances been superadded (which is evidently impossible) to the general sincere reception of the doctrine, it could not have been said with any propriety that "Christ abolished death, and brought life and immortality to light through the Gospel." The truth probably is, that as the indications of a future state which are to be found in the prophets are mostly such as will admit of an interpretation referring them to a promise of temporal deliverance, those persons would most naturally so understand them, in the first instance at least,

who were so "slow of heart" as to the prophecies respecting the Messiah, as to expect in
him a glorious *temporal* prince only; while
those who were more intelligent, and took in
the spiritual sense of the prophecies relating to
him, would be led to put the spiritual interpretation on the other also. I say, in the first
instance, because when the belief of a future
state had been introduced, from whatever
quarter, and did prevail, all who held it, would
naturally interpret in that sense whatever passages in their Scriptures seemed to confirm it.
But it does not follow that such a belief was
correct, even when supported by an appeal to
passages of Scripture which really do relate to
the doctrine in question; for if one part of a
scheme be understood literally and carnally,
and another part spiritually, the result will
be a most erroneous compound; if eternal life
be understood to be promised, but the character
and kingdom of Christ who was to bring it to
light and procure it, be misunderstood, the
faith thus formed will be essentially incorrect.
In fact, all the temporal promises of the Mosaic
law have a spiritual signification; the land of

Canaan, and the victory and prosperity, to which the Israelites were invited, are types of the future glories prepared by Christ for his followers; but then the *Law* which they were to observe as their part of the covenant, with all its sacrifices and purifications, had a corresponding spiritual signification also; being types of the redeeming sacrifice of Christ, and of the faith and holiness of heart required of his followers. Those who understood both parts literally, were right as far as they went; for the observance of the Law did literally bring these promised temporal blessings as a reward; and those also are right, and are further enlightened, who perceive the spiritual signification of *both* parts: but it is an error to couple the spiritual interpretation of one part with the literal interpretation of the other; as those of the Jews did, who imagined that eternal life was the promised reward of obedience to the Law of Moses, and who *looked for immortal happiness as the sanction of a religion to be propagated and upheld by a temporal Messiah.* This incongruous mixture of part of the shadow with part of the substance, appears to have been an error of the

Jews of our Lord's time, which not only prevented most of them from believing in him, but in great degree clung to those even who admitted his pretensions. The efficacy of the observance of the Law in procuring the blessings of the life to come, blessings which were never promised as any part of the sanction of that Law, was so inveterate a persuasion among them, that they were for superadding these extinct legal observances to their faith in Christ; and even persuaded many of the Gentile converts (among the Galatians especially) that their profession of Christianity required them to " be circumcised and keep the Law" as a condition of salvation. So far then as any of the Jews disjoined the prophetic annunciations of immortality from those relating to the spiritual kingdom of Christ, and looked for eternal rewards as earned by obedience to the Mosaic Law, so far their expectations were groundless, their faith erroneous; even though resting on the authority of such parts of Scripture as, in a different sense, do relate to the doctrine in question.

It is highly probable, however, that the belief

of a future state, as it prevailed among the Jews in our Lord's time, and for a considerable period before, was not, properly speaking, *drawn* from their Scriptures in the first instance—was not *founded* on the few faint hints to be met with in their prophets; though these were evidently called in to *support* it; but was the gradual result of a combination of other causes with these imperfect revelations. For otherwise there would surely have been some notice in the books of Ezra and Nehemiah (written after all the most important prophecies had been delivered) of so mighty a revolution having taken place in the minds of the Jews of their time, as a change from ignorance to a full conviction on so momentous a point, by a supposed decisive revelation.

Respecting the details of the rise and prevalence of the doctrine of a future state among the majority of the Jews, the scantiness of historical authority leaves us chiefly to our own conjectures. Without entering at large into a disquisition which must after all be obscured by much uncertainty, it may be allowable to suggest, that the Jews were likely to be much influenced by the *probable* arguments (for it has been admitted that there are such) which their own reason partly supplied, and which they partly learned from the neighbouring nations, with whom (and with some of the more enlightened and intelligent of them) they had much more, and much more extensive, intercourse after the captivity than before. Nor does such a supposition militate, as might at first sight be suspected, against what was formerly advanced respecting the prevailing disbelief among the heathen of the popular fables of Elysium and Tartarus, and respecting the emptiness of the pretended immortality of the soul held by philosophers, who thought that it was to be re-absorbed into the substance of the Deity, from which it had been separated, and to have no longer any distinct personal existence. For whatever their belief might be, they would be likely, in any discussion with their Jewish neighbours, to set forth either such arguments as occurred to them in favour of a future retribution, which undoubtedly was a part of the religion they professed, or such pretended proofs of the natural and necessary immortality of the soul, as their schools supplied. And such discussions we cannot but suppose must have been frequent; since the intercourse of the dispersed Jews with the Gentiles was such as to lead to the disuse of their own language, and the consequent necessity of a translation of their Scriptures into Greek. Now the Jews who claimed to be favoured with an authentic revelation of God's will, and to be his peculiar people, could not have been satisfied to rest their pretensions to such superiority, and their boast of its advantages, on the extraordinary providence under which their *ancestors* had lived, but which was withdrawn from themselves; but would be likely to set up a rival claim to that of the Pagan religions, and to produce from their Scriptures every thing that might seem to favour the hope of a future reward. And this, not insincerely; for the very circumstance of the withdrawing of that miraculous providence under which their nation had formerly lived, would lead them to the expectation of something beyond the grave to compensate the loss. God's moral government, of *their* nation at least, they were assured of, from their own past history; and if he had formerly been "a rewarder of them that diligently seek him," they would perceive an improbability of his ceasing to be so; though in this world the "just recompense of reward" was evidently no longer to be looked for. It was to be expected, therefore, that they should be more inclined to believe sincerely in a future retribution than the Pagans, who had not the same experimental assurance that the Deity is indeed the moral governor and judge of mankind.

Still, their belief, however confidently held by many of them, must have been, as has been said, fundamentally erroneous, as far as it consisted in "thinking they had eternal life in the Scriptures," held out as the reward of obedience to the Mosaic Law; which was sanctioned (as was remarked above) by no such promise. For the only just ground on which immortal happiness can be looked for, whatever some arrogant speculators have urged on the other side, is that of an express promise of it as a free gift, and not as a natural and merited recompense of virtue.

This latter notion indeed, that immortal happiness after death is the just and natural consequence of a well-spent life, (an error analogous to that of the Jews, lately mentioned,) has prevailed to a degree which, considering its utter want of foundation, either in reason or revelation, is truly surprising. A large proportion of deists, and many who admit the truth of the Gospel, though miserably ignorant of it, have either maintained, or (which is much more common, because much easier) have taken for granted and alluded to, as indisputable, the natural and necessary connexion between a virtuous life on earth and eternal happiness after death. And this is more especially the case with such as lean towards the opinion that Christianity is a mere republication of the religion of nature; a circumstance which confirms what has been just said concerning the extreme ignorance of the Gospel scheme under which these professors of Christianity labour: since if nature taught us to expect a happy eternity as the fair, natural, and well-earned reward of virtue, it would follow, that Christianity, which undoubtedly teaches no such doctrine, nor can be understood to favour it, by any one who has even a moderate acquaintance with Scripture, must be, on that very account, essentially different from natural religion, and even at variance with it.

Not only, however, is Christianity very far from being a republication of natural religion, but the notion we are speaking of is, as has been just observed, equally unfounded in reason and in revelation. As the Scriptures speak of eternal life as "the gift of God through Jesus Christ our Lord," so reason also shews, that for man to expect to earn for himself, by the practice of virtue, and claim as his just right, an immortality of exalted happiness, is a most extravagant and groundless pretension. It would indeed be no greater folly and presumption to contend, that the brutes are able by their own efforts to exalt themselves to rationality.

In the case indeed of some eminent personages of antiquity, the arrogant hope seems to have been cherished by themselves or their followers, that their great exploits and noble qualities would raise them after death into the

number of the gods; and this is precisely the
expectation we are now speaking of: for it
should be remembered, that by the term which
we translate "God," the ancient heathens understood, not, as we do, the Author and Governor
of all things, but merely a being of a nature
superior to man, perfect, happy, and immortal;
such, in short, as the Christian hopes to become
after death. Now to pretend that man is naturally capable of raising himself to this state—
of thus elevating himself into a god—is surely
no less extravagant than to suppose that a brute
is qualified to exalt itself into a rational being.
Nor did this absurdity escape the more intelligent
of the ancient heathen; their sentiments were
probably the same as the Bramin is reported to
have uttered, who on being asked by Alexander
what a man should do in order to become a god,
is said to have replied, that he must do something impossible to man. And accordingly,
the most judicious writers of antiquity make
little scruple of alluding to the temples erected
to those who were canonized as heroes, as
merely a more splendid kind of monument;
and the sacrifices offered to them, as merely a

kind of solemn commemoration, to support their posthumous fame.

Nor does the belief in a Deity, who is the moral governor of the universe, in reality alter the case so much as many seem to suppose; for if by the practice of virtue man were intitled to claim such a reward from the justice of God, he might strictly and properly be said to earn and acquire it for himself, as a labourer his wages. Men are apt indeed to speak of the justice of the Deity as leading him to the rewarding of virtue, as well as the punishing of sin, in the next world, (considering that reward and punishment as the natural consequence of each respectively,) as if the two cases were *parallel;* whereas in truth they are even *inconsistent* with each other; for a man deserves reward only from doing something *beyond his bounden duty*—something, consequently, which he would not deserve punishment for omitting. This obvious rule of justice every one assents to in human affairs: no positive rewards are proposed to men by legislators for merely fulfilling their engagements, and paying their debts; though if they fail to do so, punish-

ments are denounced; those, on the other
hand, who voluntarily devote their fortunes,
their services, or their persons, to the public
good, we consider as worthy to be rewarded
by riches, honours, or rank; while no one ever
thought of denouncing punishment for the mere
absence of such munificent liberality and ge-
nerous public spirit; which indeed would lose
their very name and character by the attempt
to make them compulsory. In no case, in
short, does justice dictate reward to be placed
on the one side of an alternative, and punishment on the other.

Now if it be admitted, (and few will go so
far as to deny it,) that *all* obedience to the
commands of our Maker is a *debt* justly due
to him,—a service his creatures are bound to
perform,—it follows, that the discharge of that
debt, by a life of perfect rectitude, would not,
in itself, entitle a man to claim any reward on
the plea of merit, except only exemption from
punishment. For as a servant (according to
the illustration used by our Lord himself) is
not *thanked* by his master for performing with
exactness his appointed task of daily labour,

so also must his disciples, as he proceeds to tell them, call themselves, even when they have done all that is required of them, "unprofitable servants, who have done but that which it was their duty to do," and who can have consequently no merit to boast.

It may be said, indeed, and with truth, that the creatures of a benevolent Deity may reasonably expect, that he should provide for the enjoyment or comfort at least of those he has called into being; as a father does for his children: and though in this world marks may be perceived of such a provision being made for the enjoyment not only of man, but of the brute creation also, (to which, be it remembered, this reasoning equally applies,) yet, since it is plain, that the goods of this world are not regularly distributed, and the best men frequently lead a life of suffering, it may be urged, that this irregularity must be rectified in a future life; in which such persons shall receive a compensation for the unmerited afflictions they have undergone in this. All this may be admitted; nor need we enquire, how far life is in general a good or an evil; or what proportion of men's sufferings may be traced to their own misconduct: let us rate, at the very highest that reason will admit, the sufferings in any supposed case, the innocence of the sufferer, and the compensation to be fairly expected ; and to what, after all, will this fair and ample compensation amount? To an eternity of exalted bliss? The idea is too extravagant to be entertained for a moment. Surely the fair compensation would fall so incalculably below this, would be such a trifle in comparison, as hardly to be worth noticing in the present argument. We see every day men submitting voluntarily, during a considerable portion of their lives, to no small amount of toil, privation, and danger, not for the certainty, but for a probability only—a chance dependent on many different contingencies— of enjoying, during the latter years of their life, such ease and comfort, wealth, prosperity, and glory, as this world has to bestow ; and, in most instances, he who refuses to do this, is censured for his indolence and folly. Now it must surely be allowed, that a *certainty* (instead of a mere contingency) of a life, approaching in length to that of the antediluvians, to be spent in the enjoyment (not of such "good things as eye hath not seen, nor ear heard, neither hath it entered into the heart of man to conceive," but) of such happiness as may be conceived in this world, would be a much fuller compensation for the greatest mass of undeserved afflictions that ever man suffered, than the attainment of such objects as men commonly aim at, (and which, after all, they are not sure of attaining,) can be reckoned, when weighed against the hardships they submit to in the pursuit. If, however, such a compensation as I have supposed should be considered too small, let it, for the argument's sake, be multiplied tenfold ; and still it will be as far as ever from bearing any proportion to that "far more exceeding and *eternal* weight of glory," which the Gospel, and the Gospel only, holds out to us, as "the *gift* of God, through Jesus Christ our Lord ;" but which man's presumptuous self-sufficiency has pretended to discover, and to claim.

An inconsiderate and hasty objector may perhaps contend, that the longest period of enjoyment would be no enjoyment at all, if known to be of limited duration; that it would be neither attractive in prospect, nor gratifying in possession, from the disturbing reflection, that it must have an end. If any one can seriously feel this as an objection, let him try to impress on the generality of mankind, as the Christian minister assiduously, and not very effectually, labours to do, the reflection, that this life must have an end, in less than a tenth part of the space allotted to the antediluvians; let him endeavour to withdraw men's attention and interest from the perishable goods and enjoyments of this world; adding also, the great *uncertainty* of them, even during the short period of our abode here; and dwelling also on the never-ending life which awaits man beyond the grave; and he will find, that, many as are the afflictions of the present life, and short, precarious, and responsible as it is, men are yet so wedded to the things of this world, that, so far from the thought of parting with them haunting us, and destroying our delight in them, it is not without a continual effort that even the best Christian can wean himself from over-attachment to the passing scene, and "set his affections on things above, not on things on the earth." And the result must be an admission, that a limited period of enjoyment, so far from being disregarded, is often even too satisfactory; that the thoughts of its termination are not apt to be even so intrusive as they ought to be.

The origin of much of the confusion of thought which has prevailed on this subject, and which has led to the groundless notion of a *claim* to immortal happiness, established by a virtuous life, is probably this; that we observe some human actions to be really and justly deserving of gratitude and reward from *other men:* being beyond what *they* had any right to demand; and hence many persons are apt to forget, that such actions cannot have a similar claim on the Almighty. Any one, for instance, who freely relieves a fellow-creature in distress, or aids him in his pursuits, is justly entitled to gratitude and reward from *him;* having done more than *that other man* had any right to demand of him: but since God *has* a strict claim upon him for the practice of every duty, no one can in his sight set up the plea of merit, or boast of his services.

Some, however, may urge, that immortal happiness, though not demanded as a right from the *justice* of God, may reasonably be hoped from his *goodness;* and that it is agreeable to his attributes to bestow it. Doubtless this is so far conformable to *what we know* of the divine attributes, that we need not be surprised at his condescending in any instance to bestow it, nor hesitate to believe, on sufficient evidence, (as the Christian does,) in his having done so. But this is far different, not only from a claim, but from a rational expectation, supposing no proof to exist of an express promise to that purpose. If a rich and liberal man freely bestows a bountiful gift on any one, he certainly performs an action suitable to his nature; but it would be strange to say, that therefore that particular person had, and that any one else has, a fair right to expect it of him. As far as we know, it is nothing inconsistent with God's nature, to confer perfection and happiness, at once, on any of his creatures; as he perhaps has on some others of them: but yet we know, that on man he has not. The immortal happiness therefore of which we are speaking, not only can be no other than a free gift, but a gift which can be reasonably expected on no other ground than that of express *promise.*

Such a promise the Christian thankfully and joyfully recognizes as held out in the Gospel; in which he finds eternal life uniformly alluded to, not as merely "brought to light" by Jesus Christ, but *procured* through his means: he came not into the world merely that his followers might *know* of this immortal life, but (as he himself declares) "that they might *have* life." The Christian Scriptures do not profess to republish, as part of the religion of nature, the doctrine that eternal happiness is the just and legitimate reward of a virtuous life; but, on the contrary, while they speak of death as the "*wages* of sin," they represent eternal life, not as the wages of obedience, but as "the *gift* of God through Jesus Christ;" a reward, indeed, dependent on obedience, but earned and merited by the righteousness and by the sacrifice of a Redeemer.

The perversion of this doctrine, by those who imagine that they may "continue in sin that grace may abound," is nothing different from

the abuse to which almost every other doctrine
of Scripture (and indeed almost every truth
ever taught) is liable. That salvation is a free
gift, through Jesus Christ, yet is prepared for
those only who obey his commandments and
walk in his steps, is in itself no more mysterious or difficult, than a multitude of cases which
occur daily, and the nature of which is readily
comprehended by every man of common sense;
because common sense is usually consulted in
the ordinary affairs of life, even by those who
lay it aside in religious questions. Every one
would judge readily and rightly in such a case,
for instance, as that of a rich and bountiful
man placing a poor labourer on a piece of
ground, which he is charged to cultivate indus-
triously and carefully, with the promise, that if
he does so, for a certain time, the land shall be
bestowed upon him in perpetuity; if not, he
shall be deprived of it. If a man placed in
this situation should suffer the ground to lie
waste, and pass his time in sloth, because he
was a dependent on another's bounty, every
one perceives that that advantage would of
course be withdrawn from him: should he, on

the other hand, diligently exert himself in till-
ing the spot of land, and then claim it, not as
a free gift, but as fairly earned by his labour,
no one would fail to censure his absurd ingra-
titude. Should a case of this kind actually
occur, it would probably be thought to present
no difficulty to any one's mind; though our
Lord's parables of the talents, and of the
pounds, which correspond so closely with it,
have so often failed to convey, as they were
designed, the same lesson'.

'It may be urged indeed, that to those who acknowledge
themselves to be *sinners*, it is of no practical consequence to
determine whether the unsinning obedience of which all men
fall short would, if practised, claim the reward of eternal life
from the justice of God. But, in fact, those who erroneously regard human virtue as naturally and in itself establish-
ing such a claim, and the redemption by Christ as needful for
man, only so far as he falls short of his duty, will generally
be found, those of them at least whose lives are the most
correct, to dislike or under-rate that Gospel, which so plainly
teaches us to plead *only* the merits of another; and to consider Christianity as *less* necessary for such men as themselves,
than for the multitude. While, on the other hand, such as
are more viciously disposed, though they may admit that it is
neither allowable nor safe to "continue in sin that grace may
abound," will yet be likely to have less abhorrence of sin, if
they conceive, that it is their *sins only* which give them an

It appears then, that whatever arguments may have been adduced, and with whatever effect, in favour of the natural and necessary *immortality* of the soul; at least the natural and necessary tendency of virtue to earn a *happy* immortality, can never have been discovered by human reason; because nothing can, properly speaking, be *discovered*, which is not *true*.

interest in the redemption: and though they may acknowledge, that with the utmost care they will not be likely to attain sinless rectitude, yet, when under the influence of temptation, they will be less practically earnest in striving to approach such perfection, from believing, that it would, if attained, supersede the necessity of Christ's sacrifice, and of itself merit salvation. Whereas, when this error is removed, we perceive the full value and importance, and also the right use, of the Gospel: and our Lord's declaration, " I am the way, the truth, and the life; no man cometh unto the Father, but by me," will be regarded neither as raising an impediment, and limiting, by an arbitrary condition, our just rights, nor yet as proposing a license, or an excuse, for sin, but as holding out a most gracious offer of an unmerited gift; and thus enforcing virtue by the strongest motives of gratitude and affection, as well as of interest. Those will surely not be the most likely to consider the righteousness of Christ as a substitute for their own, who acknowledge, that the benefits they hope for through him are such as their own righteousness, however perfect, could never have earned.

But it has been my endeavour to shew, that the arguments which human reason actually did or might suggest in favour of a future immortality, when fairly considered, as presented to the minds of such as had nothing else to proceed upon—not of such as are already believers, on other grounds—are insufficient to warrant any thing beyond a probable conjecture; and that, in fact, they very seldom produced even *that* effect. To bring the doctrine fairly within the list of truths discoverable by unaided reason, it should be shewn, first, to have not only existed, but *prevailed*, as a matter, not of conjecture, but of belief, in some nation destitute of divine revelation; 2dly, to have been believed on *sufficient grounds*; and thirdly, to have been *correctly* believed. If any one of these requisites be wanting, it cannot be properly reckoned among the doctrines of natural religion; but in truth it appears that all three of these requisites were wanting among those enlightened nations of antiquity, whose supposed knowledge of a future state is commonly appealed to: their notions were neither correct, nor well-founded, nor generally received as a matter of certain belief. And while the Gentiles were thus left in darkness, the only nation who did receive a divine revelation, had, in that, but a faint and glimmering twilight, as far as respected the glories of the world beyond the grave, till "the day-spring from on high should visit them"—till Jesus Christ should "bring life and immortality to light, through the Gospel."

To bring forward an elaborate argument to prove that he did so, considering how expressly it is asserted in the New Testament, may have appeared to some readers a superfluous task. Let them, however, but enquire of those around them, and examine the works of those who have written on the subject,—even such as not only admit the truth of Christianity, but are far from professing to regard it, or intending, in the first instance, to represent it, as a mere republication of natural religion,—and they will see that there is but too much need for asserting and maintaining the claim of "the Author and finisher of our faith," as having "brought to light" the doctrine in question. It is a claim which is often overlooked at least, even when not expressly denied; and hence one main point of evidence for the truth of Christianity is conceded to the infidel; while to the minds of believers it is presented stripped of one of its most striking peculiarities; and a most inadequate view given of its importance. The depreciation of Christianity hence resulting is perhaps not a less evil than heresy, or than infidelity itself; being one more insidious, and more incurable: for one who denies any leading doctrine of Christianity, or even the whole of it, but who yet acknowledges the *importance,* if true, of what he rejects, may at least be brought to attend to the arguments in favour of it; but far less corrigible is the error of him, who, regarding Christianity as little more than an authoritative confirmation of the religion of nature, looks upon the whole system with indifference, as a thing needed perhaps for the vulgar, but which the educated and intelligent might very well have dispensed with, and about which they need not much concern themselves.

When it is said that the view which has been taken of the doctrine of man's immortality affords an evidence for the truth of Christianity, it is not of course meant to take into the account the superior *correctness* of the Gospel accounts of a future state, as compared with the mythological fables, and philosophical theories, with which the ancients amused themselves ; *that* would of course be begging the question ; but, waiving the consideration of the *truth* of what Jesus taught on this subject, its *reception*, in spite of men's reluctance to receive it, is undeniable : and it is this that constitutes the argument 1 allude to : for let any one but compare the state of men's minds in respect to this point, before, and after, the promulgation of the Gospel ; let him estimate the opinions of the ancients, not by the hasty conjectures of prejudiced or superficial theorists, but by a careful examination of the testimony they bear to themselves ; and let him then consider the decided belief of a future state which forms a part of every modification of Christianity—of every religious system which has been founded on it, including Mahometism—let him consider, I say, the contrast thus presented ; and he will see strong reason, even from this circumstance alone, for concluding, that the Person, who could bring about this mighty revolution in the opinions of mankind, must have been a far different Being from Confucius or Socrates.

My arguments, however, as will have been seen, have been principally directed to the believers in Christianity: being anxious to protest against the error prevalent among Christians, of unduly exalting natural religion at the expense of revelation; of attributing to reason discoveries which were made, and could be made, only by the Gospel; and of thus under-rating the value of that Gospel, and dishonouring Him, who, through it, " brought life and immortality to light."

NOTES.

Note (A) page 24.

CICERO, in his epistles to his friends, in which, if
any where, he may be supposed to speak his real
sentiments, frankly avows his utter disbelief in a future
state, in one sense of the word, *i. e.* a future state
of distinct personal existence percipient of pleasure or
pain: " ut mortem, quam etiam beati contemnere de-
beamus, propterea quod *nullum sensum* esset habitura,
&c." [Epist. to L. Mescinus, Fam. Ep. l. v. ep. 21.]
And in an epistle to Toranius [l. vi. ep. 3.] he says,
" nec enim dum ero, angar ulla re, cum omni vacem
culpa; et *si non ero, sensu omnino carebo.*" This
passage will indeed bear another meaning, viz. that he
is speaking not of life or death on earth, but of the
state after death; in which, it may be said, he declares
his conviction, that if he continues to exist, his innocence
will secure him from suffering, and if he has no being at
all, he will have no sensation. The former of these would
have been indeed a sufficiently bold assumption; but the
latter, " that he who does not exist has no perception,"
is a truism which he would hardly have announced with
so much solemnity: " there needs no ghost to tell us

that." But the passage from the other epistle just quoted, in which the very same expression is used, makes it sufficiently clear that he is speaking in this also of existence and non-existence on earth; and declaring his conviction, that he who is dead has no sensation. He repeats the same sentiment in the same words [l. vi. ep. 4.] in another epistle; "si jam vocer ad exitum vitæ, non ab ea republica avellar qua carendum esse doleam, præsertim cum *id sine ullo sensu* futurum sit." And again, [l. vi. ep. 21.] "præsertim cum *omnium rerum mors sit extremum.*" And it is remarkable that he uses the very language of the Epicureans on the subject; the antidote proposed by Lucretius against the fear of death being the very same both in substance and in words :

> Scilicet haud nobis quidquam, qui *non erimus* tum,
> Accidere omnino poterit, *sensumque* movere.

Nor are these sentiments of Cicero's confined to his Epistles, though the characters of a philosopher and of an orator occasions led him sometimes to speak otherwise: in his oration for Cluentius, he avows, without disguise, a contempt, which it is evident he supposed his hearers to partake, for the notion of a future existence: "quid tandem illi mali mors attulit? nisi forte ineptiis et fabulis ducimur, ut existimemus illum apud inferos impiorum supplicia perferre, &c.—quæ si falsa sunt, *id quod omnes intelligunt,* quid ei tandem aliud mors eripuit, præter sensum doloris?"

The expressions of Seneca on the subject bear a striking resemblance to those of Cicero: "juvabat de æternitate animarum quærere, imo mehercule credere:

credebam enim facile opinionibus magnorum virorum, rem gratissimam promittentium magis quam probantium. Dabam me spei tantæ. Jam eram fastidio mihi, jam reliquias ætatis infractæ contemnebam, in immensum illud tempus et in possessionem omnis ævi transiturus: cum subito experrectus sum, epistola tua accepta, et tum *bellum somnium* perdidi." Epist. 102.

Quotations to the same effect might be multiplied without end; but these few specimens may suffice to shew how rashly the ancient philosophers have been referred to as discoverers of a future state. He who would fain " go back and walk no more with Jesus," will apply to *them* in vain for such a hope: " Lord, to whom shall we go?" the sincere Christian will exclaim; " thou hast the words of eternal life."

Note (B) *page* 29.

It is to be wished, that those who inculcate this doctrine, would be careful not to expose it, as some have done, to the scoffs of the infidel, by insisting on the restoration, at the resurrection, of the very same particles of matter which were united with the soul in this life. Supposing the doctrine to be true, neither reason nor revelation afford means for ascertaining its truth, nor for replying to the cavils brought against it. The question has been ably and copiously handled by the celebrated Mr. Locke; it will suffice therefore to observe, that, as far as we can ascertain, all the particles of a man's body are undergoing a perpetual and rapid change during his life; that which constitutes it, still

his body, being, not the identity of its materials, but
their union with the same soul, and performance of
similar functions. If (to use a familiar illustration) a
man's house were destroyed, and a kind benefactor promised to rebuild it for him, and to make it much better
than before, (for such is the promise made to true
Christians when their " earthly tabernacle shall be
dissolved,") he would not surely say that the promise
had been violated if the same precise materials were not
employed; it would suffice, that he had, as before, a
house; and one that was suitable for all the same purposes.

As for the state of the soul in the interval between
death and the general resurrection, the discussion is
unnecessary, and perhaps unprofitable; had knowledge
on this point been expedient for us, it would doubtless
have been clearly revealed; as it is, we are lost in conjecture. For ought we know, the soul may remain combined with a portion of matter less than the ten
thousandth part of the minutest particle that was ever
perceived by our senses; since "great" and "small" are
only relative. All we can be sure of is, that if the soul
be wholly disengaged from matter, and yet shall enjoy
consciousness and activity, it must be in some quite
different manner from that in which we now enjoy
them; if, on the other hand, the soul remains inert and
unconscious (as it does with respect to the seeing-
faculty, for instance, when the eyes are closed, or
blinded) till its reunion with matter, the moment of our
sinking into this state of unconsciousness, will appear to

ûs to be instantly succeeded by that of our awaking from it, even though twenty centuries may have intervened; of which any one may convince himself by a few moments' reflection.

Note (C) *page* 31.

Πᾶν τὸ ἔνυλον ἐναφανίζεται τάχιϛα τῇ τῶν ὅλων οὐσίᾳ, καὶ ϖᾶν αἴτιον εἰς τὸν τῶν ὅλων λόγον τάχιϛα ἀναλαμβάνεται. Marcus Antoninus, l. vii. c. 10. Ἐνυπέϛης ὡς μέρος. ΕΝΑΦΑΝΙΣΘΗΣΗ ΤΩ ΓΕΝΝΗΣΑΝΤΙ. l. iv. c. 14.

So Seneca, in his consolation to Marcia, daughter of Cremutius Cordus. " Mors omnium dolorum et solutio est et finis; ultra quam mala nostra non exeunt: quæ nos in illam tranquillitatem in qua *antequam nasceremur* jacuimus, reponit."

Notes (D, E) *pages* 44, 51.

Exodus xv. 26.] If thou wilt diligently hearken to the voice of the Lord thy God, and will do that which is right in his sight, and will give ear to his commandments, and keep all his statutes, I will put none of these diseases upon thee, which I have brought upon the Egyptians: for I am the Lord that healeth thee.

Chap. xx. ver. 12.] Honour thy father and thy mother, that thy days may be long, in the land which the Lord thy God giveth thee.

Chap. xxiii. ver. 20.] Behold, I send an angel before thee, to keep thee in the way, and to bring thee unto the place which I have prepared. [Ver. 21.] Beware of him, and obey his voice, provoke him not; for he will not pardon your transgressions: for my name is in him. [Ver. 22.] But if thou shalt indeed obey his voice, and do all that I speak; then I will be an enemy unto thine enemies, and an adversary unto thine adversaries. [Ver. 23.] For mine angel shall go before thee, and bring thee in unto the Amorites, and the Hittites, and the Perizzites, and the Canaanites, and the Hivites, and the Jebusites: and I will cut them off. [Ver. 24.] Thou shalt not bow down to their gods, nor serve them, nor do after their works: but thou shalt utterly overthrow them, and quite break down their images. [Ver. 25.] And ye shall serve the Lord your God, and he shall bless thy bread, and thy water; and I will take sickness away from the midst of thee. [Ver. 26.] There shall nothing cast their young, nor be barren, in thy land: the number of thy days I will fulfil. [Ver. 27.] I will send my fear before thee, and will destroy all the people to whom thou shalt come, and I will make all thine enemies turn their backs unto thee. [Ver. 28.] And I will send hornets before thee, which shall drive out the Hivite, the Canaanite, and the Hittite from before thee. [Ver. 31.] And I will set thy bounds from the Red sea even unto the sea of the Philistines, and from the desert unto the river: for I will deliver the inhabitants of the land into your hand; and thou shalt drive them out before thee.

Leviticus xxv. 17.] Ye shall not therefore oppress one another; but thou shalt fear thy God: for I am the Lord your God. [Ver. 18.] Wherefore ye shall do my statutes, and keep my judgments, and do them; and ye shall dwell in the land in safety. [Ver. 19.] And the land shall yield her fruit, and ye shall eat your fill, and dwell therein in safety. [Ver. 20.] And if ye shall say, What shall we eat the seventh year? behold, we shall not sow, nor gather in our increase: [Ver. 21.] Then I will command my blessing upon you in the sixth year, and it shall bring forth fruit for three years.

Chap. xxvi. ver. 3.] If ye walk in my statutes, and keep my commandments, and do them; [Ver. 4.] Then I will give you rain in due season, and the land shall yield her increase, and the trees of the field shall yield their fruit. [Ver. 5.] And your threshing shall reach unto the vintage, and the vintage shall reach unto the sowing time: and ye shall eat your bread to the full, and dwell in your land safely. [Ver. 6.] And I will give peace in the land, and ye shall lie down, and none shall make you afraid: and I will rid evil beasts out of the land, neither shall the sword go through your land. [Ver. 7.] And ye shall chase your enemies, and they shall fall before you by the sword. [Ver. 8.] And five of you shall chase an hundred, and an hundred of you shall put ten thousand to flight: and your enemies shall fall before you by the sword. [Ver. 9.] For I will have respect unto you, and make you fruitful, and multiply you, and establish my covenant with you. [Ver. 10.] And ye shall eat old store, and bring forth the old because of the new. [Ver. 11.] And I will set my tabernacle among you: and my soul shall not abhor you. [Ver. 12.] And I will walk among you, and will be your

God, and ye shall be my people. [Ver. 13.] I am the Lord your God, which brought you forth out of the land of Egypt, that ye should not be their bondmen; and I have broken the bands of your yoke, and made you go upright. [Ver. 14.] But if ye will not hearken unto me, and will not do all my commandments; [Ver. 15.] And if ye shall despise my statutes, or if your soul abhor my judgments, so that ye will not do all my commandments, but that ye break my covenant: [Ver. 16.] I also will do this unto you; I will even appoint over you terror, consumption, and the burning ague, that shall consume the eyes, and cause sorrow of heart: and ye shall sow your seed in vain, for your enemies shall eat it. [Ver. 17.] And I will set my face against you, and ye shall be slain before your enemies: they that hate you shall reign over you; and ye shall flee when no man pursueth you. [Ver. 18.] And if ye will not yet for all this hearken unto me, then I will punish you seven times more for your sins. [Ver. 19.] And I will break the pride of your power; and I will make your heaven as iron, and your earth as brass. [Ver. 20.] And your strength shall be spent in vain: for your land shall not yield her increase, neither shall the trees of the land yield their fruits. [Ver. 21.] And if ye walk contrary unto me, and will not hearken unto me, I will bring seven times more plagues upon you, according to your sins. [Ver. 22.] I will also send wild beasts among you, which shall rob you of your children, and destroy your cattle, and make you few in number; and your high-ways shall be desolate. [Ver. 23.] And if ye will not be reformed by me by these things, but will walk contrary unto me; [Ver. 24.] Then will I also walk contrary unto you, and will punish you yet seven times for your sins. [Ver. 25.] And I will bring a sword upon you, that shall avenge the quarrel of my covenant: and, when ye are gathered together within your cities, I will send the pestilence among you; and ye shall be delivered into the hands of the enemy. [Ver. 26.] And when I have broken the staff of your bread, ten women shall bake your bread in one oven, and they shall deliver you your bread again by weight: and ye shall eat, and not be satisfied. [Ver. 27.] And if ye will not for all this hearken unto me, but walk contrary unto me; [Ver. 28.] Then I will walk contrary unto you also in fury; and I, even I, will chastise you seven times for your sins. [Ver. 29.] And ye shall eat the flesh of your sons, and the flesh of your daughters shall ye eat. [Ver. 30.] And I will destroy your high places, and cut down your images, and cast your carcases upon the carcases of your idols, and my soul shall abhor you. [Ver. 31.] And I will make your cities waste, and bring your sanctuaries unto desolation, and I will not smell the savour of your sweet odours. [Ver. 32.] And I will bring the land into desolation; and your enemies which dwell therein shall be astonished at it. [Ver. 33.] And I will scatter you among the heathen, and will draw out a sword after you; and your land shall be desolate, and your cities waste. [Ver. 34.] Then shall the land enjoy her sabbaths, as long as it lieth desolate, and ye be in your enemies'

land; even then shall the land rest, and enjoy her sabbaths. [Ver. 35.] As long as it lieth desolate it shall
rest; because it did not rest in your sabbaths, when ye
dwelt upon it. [Ver. 36.] And upon them that are left
alive of you I will send a faintness into their hearts in
the lands of their enemies; and the sound of a shaken
leaf shall chase them; and they shall flee, as fleeing
from a sword; and they shall fall when none pursueth.
[Ver. 37.] And they shall fall one upon another, as it
were before a sword, when none pursueth: and ye shall
have no power to stand before your enemies. [Ver. 38.]
And ye shall perish among the heathen, and the land of
your enemies shall eat you up. [Ver. 39.] And they
that are left of you shall pine away in their iniquity in
your enemies' lands; and also in the iniquities of their
fathers shall they pine away with them. [Ver. 40.] If
they shall confess their iniquity, and the iniquity of their
fathers, with their trespass which they trespassed against
me, and that also they have walked contrary unto me;
[Ver. 41.] And that I also have walked contrary unto
them, and have brought them into the land of their
enemies; if then their uncircumcised hearts be humbled,
and they then accept of the punishment of their iniquity: [Ver. 42.] Then will I remember my covenant
with Jacob, and also my covenant with Isaac, and also
my covenant with Abraham will I remember; and I will
remember the land. [Ver. 43.] The land also shall be
left of them, and shall enjoy her sabbaths, while she
lieth desolate without them: and they shall accept of
the punishment of their iniquity; because, even because

they despised my judgments, and because their soul abhorred my statutes. [Ver. 44.] And yet for all that, when they be in the land of their enemies, I will not cast them away, neither will I abhor them, to destroy them utterly, and to break my covenant with them: for I am the Lord their God. [Ver. 45.] But I will for their sakes remember the covenant of their ancestors, whom I brought forth out of the land of Egypt in the sight of the heathen, that I might be their God: I am the Lord. [Ver. 46.] These are the statutes and judgments and laws which the Lord made between him and the children of Israel in mount Sinai, by the hand of Moses.

Numbers xiv. 20.] And the Lord said, I have pardoned according to thy word: [Ver. 21.] But as truly as I live, all the earth shall be filled with the glory of the Lord. [Ver. 22.] Because all those men which have seen my glory, and my miracles, which I did in Egypt and in the wilderness, have tempted me now these ten times, and have not hearkened to my voice; [Ver. 23.] Surely they shall not see the land which I sware unto their fathers, neither shall any of them that provoked me see it: [Ver. 24.] But my servant Caleb, because he had another spirit with him, and hath followed me fully, him will I bring into the land whereinto he went; and his seed shall possess it. [Ver. 28.] Say unto them, As truly as I live, saith the Lord, as ye have spoken in mine ears, so will I do to you: [Ver. 29.] Your carcases shall fall in this wilderness; and all that were numbered of you, according to your whole number, from twenty years old and upward, which have murmured against me. [Ver. 30.] Doubtless ye shall not come into the land, concerning which I sware to make you dwell therein, save Caleb the son of Jephunneh, and Joshua the son of Nun. [Ver. 31.] But your little ones, which ye said should be a prey, them will I bring in, and they shall know the land which ye have despised. [Ver. 32.] But as for you, your carcases, they shall fall in this wilderness. [Ver. 33.] And your children shall wander in the wilderness forty years, and bear your whoredoms, until your carcases be wasted in the wilderness. [Ver. 34.] After the number of the days in which ye searched the land, even forty days, each day for a year, shall ye bear your iniquities, even forty years; and ye shall know my breach of promise. [Ver. 35.] I the Lord have said, I will surely do it unto all this evil congregation, that are gathered together against me: in this wilderness they shall be consumed, and there they shall die.

Chap. xxxii. 10.] And the Lord's anger was kindled the same time, and he sware, saying, [Ver. 11.] Surely none of the men that came up out of Egypt, from twenty years old and upward, shall see the land which I sware unto Abraham, unto Isaac, and unto Jacob: because they have not wholly followed me; [Ver. 12.] Save Caleb the son of Jephunneh the Kenezite, and Joshua the son of Nun: for they have wholly followed the Lord. [Ver. 13.] And the Lord's anger was kindled against Israel, and he made them wander in the wilderness forty years, until all the generation that had done evil in the sight of the Lord, was consumed. [Ver. 14.] And behold ye are risen up in your father's stead, an increase of sinful men, to augment yet the fierce anger of the Lord toward Israel. [Ver. 15.] For if ye turn away from after him, he will yet again leave them in the wilderness; and ye shall destroy all this people.

Chap. xxxiii. ver. 55.] But if ye will not drive out the inhabitants of the land from before you; then it shall come to pass, that those which ye let remain of them shall be pricks in your eyes, and thorns in your sides, and shall vex you in the land wherein ye dwell. [Ver. 56.] Moreover it shall come to pass, that I shall do unto you, as I thought to do unto them.

Deuteronomy i. 35.] Surely there shall not one of these men of this evil generation see that good land, which I sware to give it unto your fathers. [Ver. 36.] Save Caleb the son of Jephunneh; he shall see it, and to him will I give the land that he hath trodden upon, and to his children, because he hath wholly followed the Lord. [Ver. 37.] Also the Lord was angry with me for your sakes, saying, Thou also shalt not go in thither. [Ver. 38.] But Joshua the son of Nun, which standeth before thee, he shall go in thither: encourage him: for he shall cause Israel to inherit it.

Chap. iv. ver. 1.] Now therefore hearken, O Israel, unto the statutes and unto the judgments, which I teach you, for to do them, that ye may live, and go in and possess the land which the Lord God of your fathers giveth you. [Ver. 24.] For the Lord thy God is a consuming fire, even a jealous God. [Ver. 25.] When thou shalt beget children, and children's children, and ye shall have remained long in the land, and shall corrupt yourselves, and make a graven image, or the likeness of any thing, and shall do evil in the sight of the Lord thy God, to provoke him to anger. [Ver. 26.] I call heaven and earth to witness against you this day, that ye shall soon utterly perish from off the land whereunto ye go over Jordan to possess it; ye shall not prolong your days upon it, but shall utterly be destroyed. [Ver. 27.] And the Lord shall scatter you among the nations, and ye shall be left few in number among the heathen, whither the Lord shall lead you. [Ver. 28.] And there ye shall serve gods, the work of men's hands, wood and stone, which neither see, nor hear, nor eat, nor smell. [Ver. 40.] Thou shalt keep therefore his statutes, and his commandments, which I command thee this day, that it may go well with thee, and with thy children after thee, and that thou mayest prolong thy days upon the earth, which the Lord thy God giveth thee for ever.

Chap. v. ver. 29.] O that there were such an heart in them, that they would fear me, and keep all my commandments always, that it might be well with them, and with their children for ever! [Ver. 32.] Ye shall observe to do therefore as the Lord your God hath commanded you: ye shall not turn aside to the right hand or to the left. [Ver. 33.] Ye shall walk in all the ways which the Lord your God hath commanded you, that ye may live, and that it may be well with you, and that ye may prolong your days in the land which ye shall possess.

Chap. vi. ver. 2.] That thou mightest fear the Lord thy God, to keep all his statutes and his commandments, which I command thee, thou, and thy son, and thy son's son all the days of thy life; and that thy days may be prolonged. [Ver. 3.] Hear therefore, O Israel, and observe to do it: that it may be well with thee, and that ye may increase mightily, as the Lord God of thy fathers hath promised thee in the land that floweth with milk and honey. [Ver. 10.] And it shall be when the Lord thy God shall have brought thee into the land which he sware unto thy fathers, to Abraham, to Isaac, and to Jacob, to give thee great and goodly cities, which thou buildedst not, [Ver. 11.] And houses full of all good things which thou filledst not, and wells digged, which thou diggedst not, vineyards and olive trees, which thou plantedst not; when thou shalt have eaten and be full; [Ver. 12.] Then beware lest thou forget the Lord, which brought thee forth out of the land of Egypt, from the house of bondage. [Ver. 13.] Thou shalt fear the Lord thy God, and serve him, and shalt swear by his name. [Ver. 14.] Ye shall not go after other gods, of the gods of the people which are round about you; [Ver. 15.] (For the Lord thy God is a jealous God among you) lest the anger of the Lord thy God be kindled against thee, and destroy thee from off the face of the earth. [Ver. 16.] Ye shall not tempt the Lord your God, as ye tempted him in Massah. [Ver. 17.] Ye shall diligently keep the commandments of the Lord your God, and his testimonies, and his statutes which he hath commanded thee. [Ver. 18.] And

thou shalt do that which is right and good in the sight
of the Lord: that it may be well with thee, and that
thou mayest go in and possess the good land which the
Lord sware unto thy fathers, [Ver. 19.] To cast out
all thine enemies from before thee, as the Lord hath
spoken. [Ver. 20.] And when thy son asketh thee
in time to come, saying, What mean the testimonies, and
the statutes, and the judgments which the Lord our
God hath commanded you? [Ver. 21.] Then thou shalt
say unto thy son, We were Pharaoh's bondmen in
Egypt; and the Lord brought us out of Egypt with a
mighty hand: [Ver. 22.] And the Lord shewed signs
and wonders, great and sore, upon Egypt, upon Pharaoh, and upon all his household, before our eyes:
[Ver. 23.] And he brought us out from thence, that he
might bring us in, to give us the land which he sware
unto our fathers. [Ver. 24.] And the Lord commanded us to do all these statutes, to fear the Lord our
God, for our good always, that he might preserve us
alive, as it is at this day. [Ver. 25.] And it shall be our
righteousness, if we observe to do all these commandments
before the Lord our God as he hath commanded us.

Chap. vii. ver. 12.] Wherefore it shall come to pass,
if ye hearken to these judgments, and keep, and do
them, that the Lord thy God shall keep unto thee the
covenant and the mercy which he sware unto thy
fathers: [Ver. 13.] And he will love thee, and bless
thee, and multiply thee: he will also bless the fruit of
thy womb, and the fruit of thy land, thy corn, and thy
wine, and thine oil, the increase of thy kine, and the

flocks of thy sheep, in the land which he sware unto thy fathers to give thee. [Ver. 14.] Thou shalt be blessed above all people: there shall not be male or female barren among you, or among your cattle. [Ver. 15.] And the Lord will take away from thee all sickness, and will put none of the evil diseases of Egypt, which thou knowest upon thee; but will lay them upon all them that hate thee. [Ver. 16.] And thou shalt consume all the people which the Lord thy God shall deliver thee; thine eye shall have no pity upon them: neither shalt thou serve their gods: for that will be a snare unto thee. [Ver. 23.] But the Lord thy God shall deliver them unto thee, and shall destroy them with a mighty destruction, until they be destroyed.

Chap. viii. ver. 1.] All the commandments which I command thee this day shall ye observe to do, that ye may live, and multiply, and go in and possess the land which the Lord sware unto your fathers. [Ver. 19.] And it shall be, if thou do at all forget the Lord thy God, and walk after other gods, and serve them, and worship them, I testify against you this day that ye shall surely perish. [Ver. 20.] As the nations which the Lord destroyeth before your face, so shall ye perish; because ye would not be obedient unto the voice of the Lord your God.

Chap. xi. ver. 8.] Therefore shall ye keep all the commandments which I command you this day, that ye may be strong, and go in and possess the land whither ye go to possess it; [Ver. 9.] And that ye may prolong your days in the land, which the Lord sware unto your fathers to give unto them and to their seed, a land that floweth with milk and honey. [Ver. 10.] For the land, whither thou goest in to possess it, is not as the land of Egypt, from whence ye came out, where thou sowedst thy seed, and wateredst it with thy foot, as a garden of herbs: [Ver. 11.] But the land, whither ye go to possess it, is a land of hills and valleys, and drinketh water of the rain of heaven; [Ver. 12.] A land which the Lord thy God careth for: the eyes of the Lord thy God are always upon it, from the beginning of the year even unto the end of the year. [Ver. 13.] And it shall come to pass, if ye shall hearken diligently unto my commandments which I command you this day, to love the Lord your God, and to serve him with all your heart, and with all your soul, [Ver. 14.] That I will give you the rain of your land in his due season, the first rain and the latter rain, that thou mayest gather in thy corn, and thy wine, and thine oil. [Ver. 15.] And I will send grass in thy fields for thy cattle, that thou mayest eat and be full. [Ver. 16.] Take heed to yourselves, that your heart be not deceived, and ye turn aside, and serve other gods, and worship them; [Ver. 17.] And then the Lord's wrath be kindled against you, and he shut up the heaven, that there be no rain, and that the land yield not her fruit; and lest ye perish quickly from off the good land which the Lord giveth you. [Ver. 18.] Therefore shall ye lay up these my words in your heart, &c. [Ver. 21.] That your days may be multiplied, and the days of your children, in the land which the Lord sware unto your fathers to give them, as the days of heaven upon the earth. [Ver. 22.] For if ye shall diligently keep all these commandments which I command you, to do them, to love the Lord your God, to walk in all his ways, and to cleave unto him; [Ver. 23.] Then will the Lord drive out all these nations from before you, and ye shall possess greater nations and mightier than yourselves. [Ver. 24.] Every place whereon the souls of your feet shall tread shall be yours: from the wilderness and Lebanon, from the river, the river Euphrates, even unto the uttermost sea, shall your coast be. [Ver. 25.] There shall no man be able to stand before you: for the Lord your God shall lay the fear of you and the dread of you upon all the land that ye shall tread upon, as he hath said unto you. [Ver. 26.] Behold, I set before you this day a blessing and a curse: [Ver. 27.] A blessing, if ye obey the commandments of the Lord your God, which I command you this day; [Ver. 28.] And a curse, if ye will not obey the commandments of the Lord your God, but turn aside out of the way which I command you this day, to go after other gods, which ye have not known.

Chap. xv. ver. 4.] For the Lord shall greatly bless thee in the land which the Lord thy God giveth thee for an inheritance to possess it. [Ver. 5.] Only if thou carefully hearken unto the voice of the Lord thy God, to observe to do all these commandments which I command thee this day. [Ver. 6.] For the Lord thy God blesseth thee, as he promised thee: and thou shalt lend unto many nations, but thou shalt not borrow; and thou shalt reign over many nations, but they shall not reign over thee. [Ver. 10.] Thou shalt surely give him, and thine heart shall not be grieved when thou givest unto him; because that for this thing the Lord thy God shall bless thee in all thy works, and in all that thou puttest thine hand unto.

Chap. xvi. ver. 20.] That which is altogether just shalt thou follow, that thou mayest live, and inherit the land which the Lord thy God giveth thee.

Chap. xvii. ver. 19.] And it (viz. the book of the Law, for the king's use) shall be with him, and he shall read therein all the days of his life : that he may learn to fear the Lord his God, to keep all the words of this law and these statutes, to do them : [Ver. 20.] That his heart be not lifted up above his brethren, and that he turn not aside from the commandment, to the right hand, or to the left : to the end that he may prolong his days in his kingdom, he, and his children, in the midst of Israel.

Chap. xxviii. ver. 1.] And it shall come to pass, if thou shalt hearken diligently unto the voice of the Lord thy God, to observe and to do all his commandments which I command thee this day, that the Lord thy God will set thee on high above all nations of the earth : [Ver. 2.] And all these blessings shall come on thee, and overtake thee, if thou shalt hearken unto the voice of the Lord thy God. [Ver. 3.] Blessed shalt thou be in the city, and blessed shalt thou be in the field. [Ver. 4.] Blessed shall be the fruit of thy body, and the fruit of thy ground, and the fruit of thy cattle, the increase of thy kine, and the flocks of thy sheep. [Ver. 5.] Blessed shall be thy basket and thy store. [Ver. 6.] Blessed shalt thou be when thou comest in, and blessed shalt thou be when thou goest out. [Ver. 7.] The Lord shall cause thine enemies that rise up against thee to be smitten before thy face: they shall come out against thee one way, and flee before thee seven ways. [Ver. 8.] The Lord shall command the blessing upon thee in thy storehouses, and in all that thou settest thine hand unto; and he shall bless thee in the land which the Lord thy God giveth thee. [Ver. 9.] The Lord shall establish thee an holy people unto himself, as he hath sworn unto thee, if thou shalt keep the commandments of the Lord thy God, and walk in his ways. [Ver. 10.] And all people of the earth shall see that thou art called by the name of the Lord; and they shall be afraid of thee. [Ver. 11.] And the Lord shall make thee plenteous in goods, in the fruit of thy body, and in the fruit of thy cattle, and in the fruit of thy ground, in the land which the Lord sware unto thy fathers to give thee. [Ver. 12.] The Lord shall open unto thee his good treasure, the heaven to give the rain unto thy land in his season, and to bless all the work of thine hand: and thou shalt lend unto many nations, and thou shalt not borrow. [Ver. 13.] And the Lord shall make thee the head, and not the tail, and thou shalt be above only, and thou shalt not be beneath; if that thou hearken unto the commandments of the Lord thy God, which I command thee this day, to observe and to do them: [Ver. 14.] And thou shalt not go aside from any of the words which I command thee this day to the right hand, or to the left, to go after other gods to serve them. [Ver. 15.]

But it shall come to pass, if thou wilt not hearken unto the voice of the Lord thy God, to observe to do all his commandments and his statutes which I command thee this day; that all these curses shall come upon thee, and overtake thee. [Ver. 16.] Cursed shalt thou be in the city, and cursed shalt thou be in the field. [Ver. 17.] Cursed shall be thy basket and thy store. [Ver. 18.] Cursed shall be the fruit of thy body, and the fruit of thy land, the increase of thy kine and the flocks of thy sheep. [Ver. 19.] Cursed shalt thou be when thou comest in, and cursed shalt thou be when thou goest out. [Ver. 20.] The Lord shall send upon thee cursing, vexation, and rebuke, in all that thou settest thine hand unto for to do, until thou be destroyed, and until thou perish quickly; because of the wickedness of thy doings, whereby thou hast forsaken me. [Ver. 21.] The Lord shall make the pestilence cleave unto thee, until he have consumed thee from off the land, whither thou goest to possess it. [Ver. 22.] The Lord shall smite thee with a consumption and with a fever, and with an inflammation, and with an extreme burning, and with the sword, and with blasting, and with mildew; and they shall pursue thee until thou perish. [Ver. 23.] And the heaven that is over thy head shall be brass, and the earth that is under thee shall be iron. [Ver. 24.] The Lord shall make the rain of thy land powder and dust: from heaven shall it come down upon thee, until thou be destroyed. [Ver. 25.] The Lord shall cause thee to be smitten before thine enemies: thou shalt go out one way against them, and flee seven ways before them: and shalt be removed into all the kingdoms of the earth. [Ver. 26.] And thy carcase shall be meat unto all fowls of the air, and unto the beasts of the earth, and no man shall fray them away. [Ver. 27.] The Lord will smite thee with the botch of Egypt, and with the emerods, and with the scab, and with the itch, whereof thou canst not be healed. [Ver. 28.] The Lord shall smite thee with madness, and blindness, and astonishment of heart: [Ver. 29.] And thou shalt grope at noonday, as the blind gropeth in darkness, and thou shalt not prosper in thy ways: and thou shalt be only oppressed and spoiled evermore, and no man shall save thee. [Ver. 30.] Thou shalt betroth a wife, and another man shall lie with her: thou shalt build an house, and shalt not dwell therein: thou shalt plant a vineyard, and shalt not gather the grapes thereof. [Ver. 31.] Thine ox shall be slain before thine eyes, and thou shalt not eat thereof: thine ass shall be violently taken away from before thy face, and shall not be restored to thee: thy sheep shall be given unto thine enemies, and thou shalt have none to rescue them. [Ver. 32.] Thy sons and thy daughters shall be given unto another people, and thine eyes shall look, and fail with longing for them all the day long; and there shall be no might in thine hand. [Ver. 33.] The fruit of thy land, and all thy labours, shall a nation which thou knowest not eat up; and thou shalt be only oppressed and crushed alway: [Ver. 34.] So that thou shalt be mad for the sight of thine eyes which thou shalt see. [Ver. 35.] The Lord shall smite thee in the knees, and in the legs, with a sore botch that cannot be healed, from the sole of thy foot unto the top of thy head. [Ver. 36.] The Lord shall bring thee and thy king which thou shalt set over thee, unto a nation which neither thou nor thy fathers have known; and there shalt thou serve other gods, wood and stone. [Ver. 37.] And thou shalt become an astonishment, a proverb, and a byword, among all nations whither the Lord shall lead thee. [Ver. 38.] Thou shalt carry much seed out into the field, and shalt gather but little in: for the locust shall consume it. [Ver. 39.] Thou shalt plant vineyards, and dress them, but shalt neither drink of the wine, nor gather the grapes; for the worms shall eat them. [Ver. 40.] Thou shalt have olive trees throughout all thy coasts, but thou shalt not anoint thyself with the oil; for thine olive shall cast his fruit. [Ver. 41.] Thou shalt beget sons and daughters, but thou shalt not enjoy them; for they shall go into captivity. [Ver. 42.] All thy trees and fruit of thy land shall the locust consume. [Ver. 43.] The stranger that is within thee shall get up above thee very high; and thou shalt come down very low. [Ver. 44.] He shall lend to thee, and thou shalt not lend to him: he shall be the head, and thou shalt be the tail. [Ver. 45.] Moreover all these curses shall come upon thee, and shall pursue thee, and overtake thee, till thou be destroyed; because thou hearkenedst not unto the voice of the Lord thy God, to keep his commandments and his statutes which he commanded thee. [Ver. 46.] And they shall be upon thee for a sign and for a wonder, and upon thy seed for ever.

[Ver. 47.] Because thou servedst not the Lord thy God with joyfulness, and with gladness of heart, for the abundance of all things; [Ver. 48.] Therefore shalt thou serve thine enemies which the Lord shall send against thee, in hunger, and in thirst, and in nakedness, and in want of all things: and he shall put a yoke of iron upon thy neck, until he have destroyed thee. [Ver. 49.] The Lord shall bring a nation against thee from far, from the end of the earth, as swift as the eagle flieth; a nation whose tongue thou shalt not understand. [Ver. 50.] A nation of fierce countenance, which shall not regard the person of the old, nor shew favour to the young. [Ver. 51.] And he shall eat the fruit of thy cattle, and the fruit of thy land, until thou be destroyed: which also shall not leave thee either corn, wine, or oil, or the increase of thy kine, or flocks of thy sheep, until he have destroyed thee. [Ver. 52.] And he shall besiege thee in all thy gates, until thy high and fenced walls come down, wherein thou trustedst, throughout all thy land: and he shall besiege thee in all thy gates throughout all thy land, which the Lord thy God hath given thee. [Ver. 53.] And thou shalt eat the fruit of thine own body, the flesh of thy sons and of thy daughters, which the Lord thy God hath given thee, in the siege, and in the straitness, wherewith thine enemies shall distress thee. [Ver. 54.] So that the man that is tender among you, and very delicate, his eye shall be evil toward his brother, and toward the wife of his bosom, and toward the remnant of his children which he shall leave: [Ver. 55.] So that he will not give to any of them of the flesh of his children whom he shall eat: because he hath nothing left him in the siege, and in the straitness, wherewith thine enemies shall distress thee in all thy gates. [Ver. 56.] The tender and delicate woman among you, which would not adventure to set the sole of her foot upon the ground for delicateness and tenderness, her eye shall be evil toward the husband of her bosom, and toward her son, and toward her daughter, [Ver. 57.] And toward her young one that cometh out from between her feet, and toward her children which she shall bear: for she shall eat them for want of all things secretly, in the siege and straitness, wherewith thine enemy shall distress thee in thy gates. [Ver. 58.] If thou wilt not observe to do all the words of this law that are written in this book, that thou mayest fear this glorious and fearful name, The Lord thy God; [Ver. 59.] Then the Lord will make thy plagues wonderful, and the plagues of thy seed, even great plagues, and of long continuance, and sore sicknesses, and of long continuance. [Ver. 60.] Moreover he will bring upon thee all the diseases of Egypt, which thou wast afraid of; and they shall cleave unto thee. [Ver. 61.] Also every sickness, and every plague, which is not written in the book of this law, them will the Lord bring upon thee, until thou be destroyed. [Ver. 62.] And ye shall be left few in number, whereas ye were as the stars of heaven for multitude; because thou wouldest not obey the voice of the Lord thy God. [Ver. 63.] And it shall come to pass, that as the Lord rejoiced over you to do you good, and to multiply you; so the Lord will rejoice over you to destroy you, and to bring you to nought; and ye shall be plucked from off the land whither thou goest to possess it. [Ver. 64.] And the Lord shall scatter thee among all people, from the one end of the earth even unto the other; and there thou shalt serve other gods, which neither thou nor thy fathers have known, even wood and stone. [Ver. 65.] And among these nations shalt thou find no ease, neither shall the sole of thy foot have rest: but the Lord shall give thee there a trembling heart, and failing of eyes, and sorrow of mind: [Ver. 66.] And thy life shall hang in doubt before thee; and thou shalt fear day and night, and shalt have none assurance of thy life: [Ver. 67.] In the morning thou shalt say, Would God it were even! and at even thou shalt say, Would God it were morning! for the fear of thine heart wherewith thou shalt fear, and for the sight of thine eyes which thou shalt see. [Ver. 68.] And the Lord shall bring thee into Egypt again with ships, by the way whereof I spake unto thee, Thou shalt see it no more again: and there ye shall be sold unto your enemies for bondmen and bondwomen, and no man shall buy you.

Chap. xxix. ver. 22.] So that the generation to come of your children, that shall rise up after you, and the stranger that shall come from a far land, shall say, when they see the plagues of that land, and the sicknesses which the Lord hath laid upon it; [Ver. 23.] And that the whole land thereof is brimstone, and salt, and burning, that it is not sown, nor beareth, nor any grass groweth therein, like the overthrow of Sodom, and Gomorrah,

Admah, and Zeboim, which the Lord overthrew in his anger, and in his wrath: [Ver. 24.] Even all nations shall say, Wherefore hath the Lord done thus unto this land? what meaneth the heat of this great anger? [Ver. 25.] Then men shall say, Because they have forsaken the covenant of the Lord God of their fathers, which he made with them when he brought them forth out of the land of Egypt: [Ver. 26.] For they went and served other gods, and worshipped them, gods whom they knew not, and whom he had not given unto them: [Ver. 27.] And the anger of the Lord was kindled against this land, to bring upon it all the curses that are written in this book: [Ver. 28.] And the Lord rooted them out of their land in anger, and in wrath, and in great indignation, and cast them into another land, as it is this day.

Chap. xxx. ver. 1.] And it shall come to pass, when all these things are come upon thee, the blessing and the curse, which I have set before thee, and thou shalt call them to mind among all the nations whither the Lord thy God hath driven thee, [Ver. 2.] And shalt return unto the Lord thy God, and shalt obey his voice according to all that I command thee this day, thou, and thy children, with all thine heart, and with all thy soul; [Ver. 3.] That then the Lord thy God will turn thy captivity, and have compassion upon thee, and will return and gather thee from all the nations, whither the Lord thy God hath scattered thee. [Ver. 4.] If any of thine be driven out unto the uttermost parts of heaven, from thence will the Lord thy God gather thee, and from thence will he fetch thee; [Ver. 5.] And the Lord thy God will bring thee into the land which thy fathers possessed, and thou shalt possess it; and he will do thee good, and multiply thee above thy fathers. [Ver. 7.] And the Lord thy God will put all these curses upon thine enemies, and on them that hate thee, which persecuted thee. [Ver. 8.] And thou shalt return and obey the voice of the Lord, and do all his commandments, which I command thee this day. [Ver. 9.] And the Lord thy God will make thee plenteous in every work of thine hand, in the fruit of thy body, and in the fruit of thy cattle, and in the fruit of thy land, for good: for the Lord will again rejoice over thee for good, as he rejoiced over thy fathers; [Ver. 10.] If thou shalt hearken unto the voice of the Lord thy God, to keep his commandments and his statutes which are written in this book of the law, and if thou turn unto the Lord thy God with all thine heart, and with all thy soul. [Ver. 15.] See, I have set before thee this day life and good, and death and evil; [Ver. 16.] In that I command thee this day to love the Lord thy God, to walk in his ways, and to keep his commandments and his statutes and his judgments, that thou mayest live and multiply: and the Lord thy God shall bless thee in the land whither thou goest to possess it. [Ver. 17.] But if thine heart turn away, so that thou wilt not hear, but shalt be drawn away, and worship other gods, and serve them; [Ver. 18.] I denounce unto you this day, that ye shall surely perish, and that ye shall not prolong your days upon the land, whither thou passest over Jordan to go to possess it. [Ver. 19.] I call heaven and earth to record this day against you, that I have set before you life and death, blessing and cursing: therefore choose life, that both thou and thy seed may live: [Ver. 20.] That thou mayest love the Lord thy God, and that thou mayest obey his voice, and that thou mayest cleave unto him? for he is thy life, and the length of thy days: that thou mayest dwell in the land which the Lord sware unto thy fathers, to Abraham, to Isaac, and to Jacob, to give them.

Chap. xxxi. ver. 16.] And the Lord said unto Moses, Behold, thou shalt sleep with thy fathers; and this people will rise up, and go a whoring after the gods of the strangers of the land, whither they go to be among them, and will forsake me, and break my covenant which I have made with them. [Ver. 17.] Then my anger shall be kindled against them in that day, and I will forsake them, and I will hide my face from them, and they shall be devoured, and many evils and troubles shall befal them; so that they will say in that day, Are not these evils come upon us, because our God is not among us? [Ver. 18.] And I will surely hide my face in that day for all the evils which they shall have wrought, in that they are turned unto other gods. [Ver. 29.] For I know that after my death ye will utterly corrupt yourselves, and turn aside from the way which I have commanded you; and evil will befal you in the latter days, because ye will do evil in the sight of the Lord, to provoke him to anger through the work of your hands.

Chap. xxxii. ver. 24.] They shall be burnt with

hunger, and devoured with burning heat, and with bitter destruction: I will also send the teeth of beasts upon them, with the poison of serpents of the dust. [Ver. 25.] The sword without, and terror within, shall destroy both the young man and the virgin, the suckling also with the man of gray hairs. [Ver. 46.] And he said unto them, Set your hearts unto all the words which I testify among you this day, which ye shall command your children to observe to do, all the words of this law. [Ver. 47.] For it is not a vain thing for you; because it is your life: and through this thing ye shall prolong your days in the land, whither ye go over Jordan to possess it.

Note (F) *page* 53.

In tota lege Mosaica nullum vitæ æternæ præmium, ac ne æterni quidem præmii indicium vel vestigium extat. Opinionum, quæ inter Judæos erat, circa vitam futuri sæculi discrepantia, arguit promissiones Lege factus tales esse ut ex iis certi quid de vita futuri sæculi non possit colligi. Quod et servator noster non obscure innuit, cum resurrectionem mortuorum colligit [Matt. xxii.] non ex promisso aliquo Legi additio, sed ex generali tantum illo promisso Dei, quo se Deum Abrahami, Isaaci, et Jacobi futurum sposponderat: quæ tamen illa collectio magis nititur cognitione intentionis divinæ sub generalibus istis verbis occultatæ, &c. &c. Episcopius, Inst. Theol. lib. iii. §. 1. c. 2.

Grotius distinctly maintains the same tenet: "Moses in Religionis Judaicæ institutione, si diserta Legis re-

spicimus, nihil promisit supra hujus vitæ bona, ter-
ram uberem, penum copiosum, victoriam de hostibus,
longum et valentem senectutem, posteros cum bona spe
superstites. Nam si quid est ultra, in umbris obtegi-
tur, aut sapienti ac difficili ratiocinatione colligendum
est." &c.

ESSAY II.

ON THE DECLARATION OF GOD IN HIS SON.

THAT the doctrines of man's immortality, and of the eternal reward reserved for the pious and obedient, were truly brought to light through the Gospel, I have endeavoured to establish in the First Essay. There are other peculiarities in the Christian religion, closely connected with these, which are still more frequently overlooked, (at least, overlooked *as peculiarities*,) relating to the mode in which the Gospel leads men towards the attainment of its promises, and brings them into that state of piety and of obedience, which is requisite as a preparation for immortal happiness. That piety and obedience *are* requisite to make man acceptable in God's sight, is indeed no peculiarity of the Gospel: natural religion would teach, that if there be any future state, the most likely means of making that a happy state, must be a profound reverence for the great Being on whose favour all happiness must depend, and a course of life agreeable to those moral principles which he seems to have implanted in our minds, for the regulation of our conduct: and many persons accordingly content themselves with the consideration, that piety and virtue are enforced in the Christian religion by *stronger sanctions*, (the hopes and fears of another world,) than natural religion could establish; and they notice also, perhaps, the peculiar purity of the Gospel morality; but without observing the peculiarity of the *mode* in which that piety and morality are inculcated; or rather, in which men are led to inculcate on themselves these lessons, and to acquire the requisite dispositions.

The object of the present and of the succeeding Essay will be to point out these distinguishing features: and first, that of the mode in which Christians are drawn towards God, and sentiments both of piety and of emulation of the divine goodness, implanted and cherished, by a certain peculiarity in the character of the Gospel revelation.

It is to be observed, that I am proceeding throughout on the supposition of the truth of that revelation; and without therefore adducing any *direct* evidence in support of it; though, indirectly, it may serve as a confirmation to the believer's faith, and may suggest matter of useful meditation to the sceptic, to find Christianity *distinguished*, in this and in several other remarkable particulars, both from natural religion, and from all pretended revelations; and distinguished by such marks as are favourable to its claim of coming from God.

The writings of St. John, being composed, as is generally believed, in a great measure, for the purpose of refuting the prevailing heresies of his times, and of asserting and explaining, in opposition to them, as much as is proper or possible for us to know respecting the true nature and character of Jesus Christ, are accordingly those which throw the most light on that peculiarity in the Gospel revelation which is now under consideration. In the beginning of his Gospel he tells us, [ch. i. 18.] " no man hath seen God at any time; the only-begotten Son, which is in the bosom of the Father, He hath declared him." The first clause of this passage, viz. that "no man hath seen God at any time," is an assertion so obvious and indisputable, that it seems introduced principally as a reason for the second, "the only-begotten Son, which is in the bosom of the Father, He hath declared him;" that is, the necessity of such a declaration arises from the spiritual and stupendously exalted nature of the Deity; who is not the object of any of our senses, and is very imperfectly comprehensible by our understanding.

Now it is most important to observe, that the declaration which St. John here speaks of, cannot be understood as merely an authoritative announcement of God's will, such as was made by the prophets; because the context evidently shews that he is speaking of something *peculiar* to the only-begotten Son; ἐκεῖνος ἐξηγήσατο: "He hath declared him," or rather, with still more propriety, "*it is He that hath declared him:*" this *declaration* therefore does not refer to a mere *message* sent from God, but to a *manifestation* of God himself in Jesus Christ: which St. John has just above described by saying, "the Word was made flesh, and dwelt among us." He came, not merely as a prophet *sent from* God, but as " Emmanuel, God *with us*." This view of the declaration or revelation which He made of God, is strikingly confirmed by numerous other passages in the sacred writings: He says of Himself, " he that hath seen me, hath seen the Father." St. Paul describes the incarnation, by saying, "God was *manifest* in the flesh;" and that Christ was the brightness of his glory, ἀπαύγασμα τῆς δόξης, and the express image of his person, χαρακτὴρ τῆς ὑπόστασεως. Now that the divine nature of Christ is implied in these passages, though sufficiently clear, it is not my present object to point out; but that they represent the incarnation as a certain kind of *revelation, display*, or manifestation, to men, of the divine nature. In what manner, and for what purpose, this manifestation was effected, is the object of our present enquiry.

But in order to keep clear of even the suspicion of that most unchristian and dangerous fault, *presumption*, it will be necessary to premise two remarks; first, that we are enquiring, not why the incarnation *took place*, but why it was *made known to us:* now there is a wide difference between two things, which nevertheless the inattentive are apt to confound together; I mean, between enquiring into the reasons of the divine counsels themselves, and enquiring into the reasons of their being *made known* to us : the former is in very many cases both a fruitless and a presumptuous enquiry, because it relates frequently to unknown parts of the creation, and to the attributes and operations of the divine mind, which are beyond our clear comprehension; whereas, to enquire why certain doctrines are *revealed* to *us*, can hardly be a blameable, and will generally be a profitable, often indeed a necessary, enquiry, because *this* relates to our own minds—to the practical effect intended to be produced on ourselves. For example, why the sacrifice of Christ was necessary for our redemption, is a mystery beyond the reach of our present faculties; and all attempts fully to explain it have served only to excite a prejudice against the doctrine, and to expose the weakness of arrogant speculation : but to consider why this sacrifice of

Christ was *announced* to mankind, is both allowable and necessary; it was doubtless for the purpose of exciting our gratitude, confidence, love, and obedience, towards him; together with a deep abhorrence of sin, which needed so mighty an expiation.

So also in the present case, we dare not presume to determine why God thought fit to take our nature upon him in Jesus Christ. But why he thought fit to *reveal* this incarnation—to announce himself as the eternal " Word made flesh"—is what it cannot but behove us to know.

The other caution to be observed is, that in those cases where we can perceive *something* of the purposes which God has in view, we are not thence to conclude that we know them *all:* many great objects may be comprehended in each of God's dispensations; though but a very small part of these objects be as much as is sufficient, and perhaps possible, for us, in our present state, to understand. We are sure that the sun gives light and heat to this world; and many ignorant savages perhaps conclude from thence, that it was created for no other purpose; doubtless we are as much called on for gratitude as if the case were so; but we are well assured, that many other planets partake of the same advantages; and we should be very much to blame, were we to conclude positively that even this is the sole, or indeed the principal, purpose for which the sun was created[a]. So in the present case also, whatever benefits to mankind we may perceive from the manifestation of God in the flesh, we have no right to infer, that there may not be other, and even greater, objects effected by it, of which, for the present at least, we must remain ignorant.

With these cautions carefully kept in mind, we may proceed, with due reverence, to enquire, for what purposes we are taught by Scripture to believe in the incarnation of God in Christ Jesus, and to regard *that* as a manifestation of God to his creatures. We shall find good reason for concluding, that it was designed, in part at least, for the purpose of

[a] To have ascertained and to perceive *a* reason for any thing that God has done, is far different from perceiving *the* reason; though the two are often confounded.

leading men both to piety and to morality, by a method admirably adapted to that purpose, and which is absolutely peculiar to Christianity : viz. by first bringing down more to the level of our capacity the moral attributes of the Deity, and thus better engaging our affections on the side of devotion ; and secondly, by exhibiting a perfect and exalted model of human excellence. Both these objects are effected by the mysterious union of the divine and human natures ; the divine "Word was made flesh," to lead us to affectionate piety ; and "the manhood was taken into God," to teach us Godlike virtue.

The few remarks which I propose to offer on each of these points, though very far from exhausting the subject, may be sufficient to suggest, to such as are disposed to pursue it, a train of pleasing and profitable meditation.

First then, with respect to piety : (or whatever other term may be employed, to denote collectively the sentiments felt or expressed by men towards a Supreme Being :) it is indeed undeniable, that the works of creation clearly indicate a Contriver of stupendous power and

wisdom, whose observation we can never hope
to elude, nor to resist his will : and we cannot
but acknowledge his goodness, in bestowing
on his creatures all the benefits they enjoy,
notwithstanding our inability to explain those
appearances of evil which present themselves.

But though it is easy to say that we ought to
love and worship, as well as reverence and
fear, the Supreme Being, yet nothing is in fact
more difficult for such a creature as man, sur-
rounded too, as he is, by gross material objects, and necessarily occupied in worldly pursuits, than to lift up his thoughts and affections
to God. A Being, whose nature is so incompre-
hensible that our knowledge of him is chiefly
negative; of whom we know, not so much
what He is, as what He is *not*, it is difficult to
make even a steady object of thought: now we
believe that God is a *spirit*; but we have a
very faint notion of the nature of a spirit,
except that it is *not* a body: God is *eternal*;
but we are bewildered with the very idea of
Eternity, of which we only know that it is
without beginning, and *without* end : we say
that the divine attributes are *infinite*; i. e.

not bounded, *unlimited.* And even where our knowledge of God extends beyond mere negatives, we cannot but perceive, on attentive reflection, that the attributes assigned to the Deity must in reality be such, in him, as the ordinary sense of those same terms, when applied to men, can but very faintly shadow out[b].

[b] " We ought to remember, that the descriptions which we frame to ourselves of God, or of the divine attributes, are not taken from any direct or immediate perceptions that we have of him or them ; but from some observations we have made of his works, and from the consideration of those qualifications, that we conceive would enable us to perform the like. Thus observing great order, conveniency, and harmony in all the several parts of the world, and perceiving that every thing is adapted, and tends to the preservation and advantage of the whole ; we are apt to consider, that we could not contrive and settle things in so excellent and proper a manner without great wisdom ; and thence conclude that God, who has thus concerted and settled matters, must have wisdom : and having then ascribed to him wisdom, because we see the effects and result of it in his works, we proceed and conclude that he has likewise foresight and understanding, because we cannot conceive wisdom without these, and because if we were to do what we see he has done, we could not expect to perform it without the exercise of these faculties.

" And it doth truly follow from hence, that God must either have these or other faculties and powers equivalent to them,

But the difficulty is still greater, when we attempt to set our *affections* on this awful and

and adequate to these mighty effects which proceed from them. And because we do not know what his faculties are in themselves, we give them the names of those powers, that we find would be necessary to us, in order to produce such effects, and call them wisdom, understanding, and foreknowledge: but at the same time we cannot but be sensible that they are of a nature altogether different from ours, and that we have no direct or proper notion or conception of them. Only we are sure that they have effects like unto those that do proceed from wisdom, understanding, and foreknowledge in us: and when our works fail to resemble them in any particular, as to perfection, it is by reason of some want or defect in these qualifications.

" Thus our reason teaches us to ascribe these attributes to God, by way of resemblance and analogy to such qualities or powers as we find most valuable and perfect in ourselves.

" If we look into the holy Scriptures, and consider the representations given us there of God or his attributes, we shall find them generally of the same nature, and plainly borrowed from some resemblance to things with which we are acquainted by our senses. Thus when the holy Scriptures speak of God, they ascribe hands, and eyes, and feet to him: not that it is designed that we should believe that he has any of these members according to the literal signification: but the meaning is, that he has a power to execute all those acts, to the effecting of which these parts in us are instrumental: that is, he can converse with men as well as if he inconceivable Being;—to address as a tender parent, Him, who has formed out of nothing,

had a tongue and mouth; he can discern all that we do or say as perfectly as if he had eyes and ears; he can reach us as well as if he had hands and feet; he has as true and substantial a being as if he had a body; and he is as truly present every where as if that body were infinitely extended. And in truth, if all these things, which are thus ascribed to him, did really and literally belong to him, he could not do what he does near so effectually, as we conceive and are sure he doth them by the faculties and properties which he really possesses, though what they are in themselves be unknown to us." King's Sermon, §. iv. p. 6—10. That I do not admit Dr. King's application of his principles, to the explanation of the difficulty of reconciling the divine Prescience with human Freedom, is necessary to be mentioned, for the sake of such of my readers only as have not seen the notes accompanying my edition of his Sermon, and may be led to suppose the contrary, from a statement in a note to one of Mr. Davison's Lectures on Prophecy, in which he attributes to me the adoption of the Archbishop's views on that point. That statement originated entirely in a mistake; as the author (whom I well knew to be incapable of wilful misrepresentation) candidly acknowledged to me.

My reasons for differing from Archbishop King on this point are fully stated in the notes just mentioned. Of the value and importance of his general principles I am more and more convinced; especially, as more than four years have elapsed since the work has been recalled to public notice, both and could annihilate in a moment, countless myriads, perhaps, of worlds besides our own; and to whom " the nations are but as the drop of a bucket, and the small dust of a balance ;"— to offer our tribute of praise and obedience to Him, who can neither be benefited nor hurt by us;—to implore favour and deprecate punishment from Him, who has no passions, nor wants, as we have ;—to confess our sins before Him, who is exempt not only from all sin, but from all human infirmities and temptations ;— and, in short, to hold spiritual intercourse with One, with whom we can have no sympathy, and of whom we can with difficulty form any clear conception.

And this difficulty is not diminished, but rather increased, in proportion as man advances in refinement of notions, in cultivation

by Dr. Copleston's commendation and masterly analysis of it, (in the notes to his " Discourses on Predestination,") and by the new edition of it, published in consequence; in the notes to which, as well as in the analysis just mentioned, Dr. King's main principles have been explained and supported by reasons, against which nothing has, in all that time, been advanced that deserves the name of argument.

of intellect, and in habits of profound philosophical reflection; and thus becomes less gross
in his ideas of the Supreme Being. To the
dull and puerile understandings of a semi-
barbarous nation, such as the Israelites at the
time of Moses, many of the circumstances just
mentioned would be less likely to occur, than
to those of a more enlightened people; and an
habitual and practical piety would accordingly
have been more easy of attainment by them,
while favoured, as they were, with frequent
sensible divine interpositions of various kinds,
and continually addressed by prophets in the
name of the Lord, Jehovah, the tutelary God
of their nation, than for men of more enlarged
minds, and more thoughtful habits, *not* favoured with the Gospel revelation.

These impediments to devotion it is probable
St. John had in mind, when he said, " No man
hath seen God at any time;" and that he conceived the " declaration" of God, by Jesus
Christ, was calculated, not indeed wholly to
remove these impediments, but so far to moderate and lower them, as to leave no insuper-
able difficulty to a willing mind.

To the causes which have been enumerated it is to be attributed, that the religion of those who are called philosophers, whose speculations respecting the Deity have been accounted the most refined and exalted, has always been cold and heartless in its devotion; or rather has been nearly destitute of devotion altogether.

On the other hand, the great mass of mankind, from the same cause, have in all ages and countries shewn a disposition to address their prayers not to the Supreme Creator immediately, but to some angel, demi-god, subordinate deity, or saint, (as is the practice of the Romish Church,) whom they suppose to approach more to their own nature, to form a sort of connecting link between God and man, and to perform for them the office of Intercessor. Thus while the one class are altogether wanting in affectionate devotion, the other direct it to an improper object; giving that worship to the creature which is due only to the Creator. A preventive for both these faults is provided, in that manifestation of God in Jesus Christ, which affords us such a display of the divine attributes, as, though very faint and imperfect, is yet the *best* calculated, considering what human nature is, to lead our affections to God. When Christ fed a multitude with five loaves, He made not indeed a greater nor a more benevolent display of power, than He does in supporting from day to day so many millions of men and other animals as the universe contains; but it was an instance far better calculated to make an impression on men's minds of his goodness and parental care. I speak not now of this miracle as an *evidence* of his pretensions; for that purpose would have been answered as well by a miracle of destruction; but of the peculiar *beneficent* character of it. So also, in healing the sick, raising the dead, and preaching to the people; though these are not greater acts of power and goodness than the creation of the world and all things in it, yet they are what the minds of most men, at least, can more steadily dwell upon, and which, therefore, are most likely to affect the heart.

Many, it is true, of the qualities which our Lord displayed, such as his patience under provocation, and fortitude against pain and danger, are such as can belong to Him in his human nature alone, and can present us but a very faint shadow of the attributes of God, considered as such; but still these are attributes of one and the same *Person*, in whom we believe the divine and human natures to have been united; though we cannot comprehend that union, any more than indeed we can that of the human soul and body: and they are well fitted to fix our affections on that Person: and if any one should contend, by drawing nice metaphysical distinctions, that this is not properly to be called the love of God, it is at least the nearest approach to it of which our nature is capable.

If we cannot endure steadily to gaze on the sun, but prefer contemplating his brightness as reflected from the objects on the earth, much more may we expect, that the splendour of the Divine Being should be too dazzling for mortal gaze; that it should be necessary for his brightness to be veiled in flesh, in order to enable us to contemplate it in the best manner that, for us, is possible; and that we should have a better notion of Him by viewing this radiation of his glory, [ΑΠΑΥΓΑΣΜΑ ΤΗΣ ΔΟΞΗΣ,] than by straining our weak faculties in attempting to comprehend Him as He is. Our views indeed on this awful subject must after all be indistinct, confused, and imperfect; but if they are better than we could otherwise have attained, and are the utmost that we can or need attain, the object is sufficiently accomplished.

If indeed, as is notoriously the fact, our only notions of the divine attributes, and our terms for expressing them, are, and always must be, borrowed from such human qualities as have the most analogy to them, it seems to follow inevitably, that the more excellent man would give us ever the more adequate notion of the divine excellence; and consequently, that the life of that man who was altogether perfect, by union with the Godhead, must afford us the very best idea (however imperfect that best may be) that we can attain, of the moral attributes of God. Moreover, our Lord was subject to all the wants, infirmities, and temptations, incident to his and our human nature[c];

---

[c] It should be remembered, that we are not exalting the character of Jesus, if we regard Him as naturally destitute of such feelings as ambition, love of glory, patriotism, and other

and suffered on the cross for our redemption; this calls for our sympathy, as well as reverence and gratitude; and the affectionate attachment

such natural propensities, as are not in themselves sinful; nor could it, in that case, have been said with truth, that He " was *in all points tempted* like as we are." No doubt the offer of temporal dominion, to a descendant of the royal house of David, together with the eager reception this would have ensured Him with his countrymen, who were anxiously looking for such a Messiah, and the glory and pleasure of delivering them from a foreign yoke, constituted a real and strong temptation; especially when the alternative was rejection by his brethren, insult, persecution, and ignominious death. May not this offer have been pressingly renewed just at the time of his betrayal? and may not this temptation have been the " cup" which He prayed might be removed from Him? for we are told, (Heb. v. 7.) that " he offered up prayers and supplications with strong crying and tears, unto Him that was able to save Him from death, and *was heard*, in that He feared:" now we know that He was *not* saved from the death on the cross; it must have been something else therefore from which He prayed for deliverance, and *was heard*. And the Evangelist tells us, that " there appeared unto Him an angel from heaven *strengthening* Him."

Certainly it appears more probable, that the plot laid by Judas Iscariot (who could not be ignorant of his Master's supernatural powers) was for driving Him to assume a temporal dominion, than that it was directed against his life. See a dissertation on this subject in " The Night of Treason," by the Rev. F. Thruston.

thus so naturally generated, will adhere (if I may so express myself) to the divine nature of the Saviour also. And when we worship Him, though we worship Him not as man, but as God, still it will give an affectionate fervor to our devotions, to have an habitual remembrance, that this very God was also man, deigning for our sakes to be " made flesh, and dwell among us,"" taking upon Him the form of a servant, and humbling Himself even unto the death of the cross." Undoubtedly it was in this point of view that St. Paul intended the doctrine of the Incarnation to be considered, when he said, [Heb. iv. 15, 16.] " We have not an high priest which cannot be touched with the feeling of our infirmities, but was in all points tempted like as we are, yet without sin. Let us therefore come boldly to the throne of grace, that we may obtain mercy, and find grace to help in time of need." Observe also how in the Epistle to the Colossians he presents to our view the divine and the human attributes of the Saviour almost simultaneously ; " in whom," says he, " we have redemption *through his blood*, even the forgiveness of sins ; who is the image of the invisible God, the first-born of every creature, (πρωτότοκος πάσης κτίσεως, born *before* all creatures,) for *by Him were all things created*, that are in heaven, and that are in earth, visible and invisible." Col. i. 14, 15, 16.

It is not necessary, in an argument addressed to persons who are supposed acquainted with the Scriptures of the New Testament, to dwell as fully as might be done on those innumerable points in the character and conduct of our Saviour, which may be said with literal propriety to display *divine* excellence; and that, in the most impressive and at the same time in the most amiable form. The contemplation indeed of that character should be an habitual study to every Christian. It will have been sufficient merely to direct the attention of a believer in the Gospel to the point in question,—the advantage with respect to piety which was intended to accrue from this declaration of God in Christ; by its shewing us, not indeed the divine Being as he is, but " the express image," or stamp and impression of Him, (χαρακτὴρ τῆς ὑποστάσεως)—by exhibiting, though a very imperfect, yet a more impressive and endearing picture of the moral attributes of God than we could in any other way attain ; and thus drawing our whole heart and affections towards Him.

II. Another advantage which was stated to have been probably designed in exhibiting to man the stupendous work of the Incarnation, is, the proposing a perfect model for our imitation. It is an old and well-established maxim, that men learn better from example than from precept ; but the difficulty is to find an example fit for imitation. Mere human models are all, more or less, imperfect ; and though it is undeniable, that very great benefit may be derived from them, if we are careful to point out, and warn men against their faults, and by assembling together many different characters of great worth, to provide that the deficiencies of each may be supplied by others ; yet still there must always be a certain degree of danger in copying even the best men. The faults and the virtues of each individual are in general so intimately blended, and, as it were, fit together so readily, that it is not easy to avoid the one, while aiming at the other. The faults of one whom we regard as a great and good man, become endeared and ennobled in our eyes by a union with so much virtue: we are apt to take such a favourable view of them, as leads us to excuse them in ourselves; and perhaps ultimately even to admire and copy them; " Decipit exemplar vitiis imitabile," is accordingly no less trite a maxim than that which recommends the study of approved models.

It was probably for this reason that the Stoics held forth as a pattern their ideal wise man. For the Sapiens—the Wise-man, or perfectly good and happy character, whom these philosophers delineated—was not one whom they themselves pretended to have ever actually existed. This circumstance, by the way, (though such is undoubtedly the fact,) has been overlooked by many; who have thence charged them with arrogant pretensions to perfect virtue, which it does not appear they ever made. Their object seems to have been, to avoid on the one hand the comparative flatness and tediousness of abstract descriptions, and, on the other hand, the errors to be dreaded from the imperfection of human models. And they certainly judged rightly in thinking, that however inevitable it may be that men should have defects, the pattern which is proposed to them should have none; for, far as they will still fall short of perfection, they will thus approach much nearer to it than if they had copied a defective model.

This method, however, of leading men to morality, though perhaps the best that in their situation they could have devised, laboured under a very important defect: I speak not of the *blemishes* in the ideal Wise-man they described; though the character which they meant for a perfect one, was, according to the more correct principles now established, very far from perfect; still it is conceivable that it *might* have been so: let us then suppose it completely unexceptionable; still it is *ideal;* it wants the power of inspiring that interest and sympathy, that affectionate reverence, that emulation, which a really existing *person* can alone inspire; and being represented to us only by general *descriptions,* it takes even less hold of the mind than the fictitious hero of a drama, who is represented as performing distinct individual actions; though we know that both are alike creatures of the imagination; which have therefore but a very faint effect in exciting us to imitation. An ideal model, in short, is but one short step removed from abstract moral precept: real human examples, on the contrary, are unsafe, from their imperfection. Both may do some service, but both leave much to be desired.

But if, while some of the ancient moralists were employed in recounting the actions, and holding forth the examples, of really existing illustrious men, to stimulate the emulation of their hearers,—and while others were pointing out, in the grave and lofty descriptions of the philosopher, or the vivid representations of the poet, an ideal exemplar of perfect excellence; a man exhibited such as men *should* be, not such as they are,—what would these sages, I say, have thought, had they been assured on sufficient authority that such a man had actually appeared on earth; not having his virtues tarnished with defects, like the heroes of their histories; not a phantom of imagination, like the Persons of their theatre, or the Wise-man of their schools; but a real, living, sublime, and faultless model of god-like virtue? Surely they would have acknowledged with one voice, that such a character, and such a one only, was exactly suited to their wishes, and to the wants of their hearers: if they were at all sincere in their professions, they would have hailed with rapture the announcement of his existence; but would have wondered, at the same time, and doubted, how human nature could ever have attained this pitch of excellence. We might have answered them, "human nature by itself is indeed far too weak for the task; but in Christ the divine nature was united to it; in Him "dwelt all the fulness of the Godhead bodily:" the Deity was ever present in an especial manner to direct and support his human soul, and thus presented to his creatures a perfect pattern, which, through the promised aid of the Holy Spirit, they may copy; that by imitating the divine excellence, as far as it is possible for a creature to do so, we may become, as Christ himself expresses it, "like unto our Father which is in heaven," and be thus fitted for enjoying a more near approach to his presence in a better state: that we also (as St. Paul says) may be called " sons of God, brethren, and joint-heirs of Christ," and partakers of his glory. " Beloved," (says St. John,) "now are we the sons of God; and it doth not yet appear what we shall be; but we know that when He shall appear, we shall be like unto Him; for we shall see Him as He is." Behold here then (we might exclaim) a truly godlike man, far surpassing your historical or fabulous heroes! Behold here your imaginary Wise-man exemplified in real life! what you have described, that, and much more, He has performed; for He has corrected in actual practice, the errors of your description, and has realized a nobler and more lovely picture of virtue than even your conceptions ever reached.

It would be unnecessary, I trust, were it possible within reasonable limits, to enter into a detailed examination of the virtues of Christ's character; every Christian who deserves the name, makes it his attentive study; and those who have learned the most of it, are ever the most desirous and the most capable of learning yet more. Many valuable writers have treated of the subject; but the Gospels themselves (as those very writers would be the first to admit) will teach more of the imitation of Christ than all other books together. Each man may do more for himself in this study than the ablest theologian can do for him. He will find in every page such active yet unpretending benevolence—such exalted generosity and self-devotedness—such forbearing kindness and lowliness, combined with dignity—such earnest and steady, yet calm and considerate, zeal—such quiet and unostentatious fortitude—such inflexible yet gentle resolution—that he must acknowledge with the Jewish officers, "never man spake like this man;" never did man, he will add, act like this man; "truly," as the Centurion exclaimed, "this was a righteous man; truly this was the Son of God:" it was " Emmanuel, God with us." And if the student's own heart be not in fault, his character will not fail to receive some tincture from the virtue he is contemplating.

Whatever may be our station in life, or peculiar circumstances, we shall still find, that

Jesus Christ has " left us an ensample that we should follow his steps," because the principle of devoted obedience to God, love towards man, and abjuration of all selfish objects, is one which is called for, and must be put in practice, in every situation. Besides which, it is very observable, that while all the illustrious characters which are usually held up to our imitation are persons who occupied such exalted stations, that their lives afford but little instruction to those in humbler and more private situations, (that is, in fact, to the great mass of mankind;) our Saviour's life, on the contrary, though He had so high an office to execute, yet from the humble station in which He appeared, contains lessons for every description of mankind.

It appears then, that Jesus Christ has " declared" God to man, not as a prophet merely, but as (what St. Paul calls him in the Epistle to the Colossians) " the Image of the invisible God;"—not merely by announcing the divine will, but by manifesting, as far as our feeble capacities will permit, the divine glory, and shadowing forth the attributes of the invisi-

ble and unsearchable God.   And this for two
purposes most important to mankind ; first, by
a softened and endearing, as well as impressive, manifestation of the Deity, to aid and
exalt our piety, engaging our affections in the
cause of religion ; and, secondly, by a bright
example of superhuman virtue, seconded by
the promise of spiritual aid, to instruct and encourage us in our duty—to illuminate and direct
our Christian course—to purify and to elevate
our nature.   The one purpose, in short, may be
said to have been, to bring down God to Man ;
the other, to lift up Man towards God.

Now if this view of the subject be correct, it
must be admitted that the method adopted in
the Gospel for leading men to piety and to
morality, is something altogether peculiar to
Christianity ; and it is one of those peculiarities
which, as was formerly remarked, men are too
apt to overlook or to undervalue. I speak not
now of those who distinctly deny the divinity
of our Lord ; but it is, I apprehend, not uncommon for those who assent to the *truth* of
that doctrine, to pass by unheeded the important purposes for which it was *revealed ;* and

thence to lose sight of that striking peculiarity in the Christian religion which results from that revelation, and which it has been the object of this Essay to point out.

The Incarnation, as an abstract speculative point, they are aware is taught in the Gospel, and only in the Gospel; but the Incarnation, as the basis of the Christian's worship, and of the Christian's obedience, they are too apt entirely to disregard. They content themselves with perceiving, generally, that all religions whatever inculcate piety to God, and virtuous conduct; and fail to observe, that in the very points which are, thus far, common to all, Christianity is strikingly distinguished from the rest: the *mode* in which it leads us to that piety and virtue, is altogether peculiar to it.

Another circumstance of peculiarity, however, in that mode, remains to be noticed. It is evident, that in order to form a virtuous character it is requisite not only that a perfect standard be set before us, (such as the model which the Gospel holds out for our imitation,) but also that adequate motives be supplied. And though the emulation which the contemplation of an admirable model is calculated to inspire is, to a certain degree, a motive, it is not alone sufficient. The rewards and punishments of the next world, as declared in the Gospel, have been already mentioned as furnishing one most powerful motive; but there is another besides this—an appeal to the feelings, not merely to the judgment—a motive of affection, not of mere interest—the introduction of which forms a strikingly distinguishing feature of Christianity; and this peculiarity will form the subject of the next Essay.

ESSAY III.

ON LOVE TOWARDS CHRIST AS A MOTIVE TO OBEDIENCE.

IF the Gospel had merely given us the assurance of a future retribution, teaching us at the same time to look for immortal happiness through faith in the merits and sacrifice of our Redeemer, (not as the well-earned reward of our own virtue,) yet requiring us to practise virtue nevertheless, as an indispensable condition, and, in addition to moral precepts, holding out a model of superhuman excellence to excite our emulation—it would have been distinguished indeed by many important peculiarities, and it would have contained *every* incentive to holiness of life that some Christian readers attribute to it. But in fact it does much more. The rewards and punishments of the next world do indeed furnish a strong incitement to the practice of duty; the moral precepts of the

Scriptures, and still more the example of
Christ, help us to ascertain what our duty is;
and the emulation which such a model naturally inspires, affords an additional incentive:
but this is not all. It is possible for men to
emulate the virtues of one who is personally an
utter *stranger* to them; and to profit by his
example, though he have no connection with
them, no care or knowledge whether they
imitate him or not. But they are much more
strongly incited to do this, if they know that
the person in question does take an interest in their welfare—is their greatest benefactor—and on that ground calls on them to
conform to his precepts, and to tread in his
steps. And this we shall find is the case, in
a most remarkable degree, in the religion of
Jesus Christ. One of its most striking peculiarities is, its continual appeal to the affections;
its introducing as a principal motive to obedience, love towards our heavenly Master. He
appeared as " God with us," and as partaking
of our nature, with a view both to display to us
an exalted and perfect model of goodness, and
also to awaken in us more effectually those

feelings of pious and affectionate attachment, which it would be less easy to entertain towards God, considered as the invisible Author and Governor of the universe. In beautiful conformity with this plan, these feelings are required to manifest themselves in a duteous regard to his will; and on these we are taught that the moral regulation of our lives is to be founded. " If ye love me, keep my commandments," is our Lord's injunction, as reported by St. John in his Gospel^a; "and this is love," (says the same Evangelist in his general Epistle,) " that we walk after his commandments." Here we have set before us at once the best principle, and the best application of it; the purest motive, and the most perfect practice: here, in short, we are told both what our conduct ought to be, and from what source that conduct ought to spring. It is undeniable that the very best actions are of no value, unless they proceed from a right principle; and again, that a right principle is utterly barren and unprofitable, unless it lead us to right

---

^a Chap. xiv. 15.

practice. The Gospel supplies us both with the motive, and the rule; " If ye love me, keep my commandments." This precept therefore is to be considered in two points of view : first, that the love of Christ is the *proper ground* of our obedience—the *reason why* we ought to keep his commandments: secondly, that the proper effect, and sure test, of our love for Christ, is, the keeping of his commandments.

On each of these points many have fallen into dangerous mistakes; and some indeed have entirely lost sight of both. Persons may be found, who profess a most fervent and zealous love for their Redeemer, yet are so far from giving proof of their love by keeping his commandments, that they seem to consider the very warmth of their feelings—their religious fervor—as an excuse for the carelessness of their practice, and as affording them a kind of license for indulging their sinful inclinations; forgetful of the plain warning given by Christ himself, " Not every one that saith unto me, Lord, Lord, shall enter into the kingdom of heaven; but he that doeth the will of my Father which is in heaven." And this perver-

sion of Christianity by some persons has had
the effect of inspiring others with an aversion
or contempt for all sentiments of affectionate
piety ;—of bringing into disrepute altogether
the Gospel motive of love towards the Redeemer, as savouring of dangerous fanaticism,
and leading to the substitution of enthusiastic
feelings, for a virtuous life. But the perversity
of man is no ground either for censuring, or for
rejecting, or for seeking to alter and new-
model, the word of God ; which sufficiently
guards those who will but study it fairly,
against such abuse of the doctrine before us.
Indeed, one of the most striking peculiarities
of our religion, consists in the strong contrast
which the preaching of our Lord and his followers presents, in this respect, to most of the
systems of religion, which have been devised
by men. Rich offerings could not, with Him,
as among the pagans, make amends for a sinful
life : neither painful austerities, nor splendid
festivals, were by Him allowed to compensate
for the want of purity of heart, and subdued
passions ; no zeal in his service, nor readiness
even to shed their blood in his cause, would

excuse his followers, as it would those of Mahomet, from the performance of their moral duties. "Why," says He, "call ye me Lord, Lord, and do not the things which I say?" and He declares, that even those who had wrought miracles in his name would be disavowed by Him, if "workers of iniquity."

There are others, on the contrary, driven, probably, (as has just been observed,) by their dread of the extreme above mentioned, into the opposite, who, in the sentiments they utter, or in the conduct of their lives, seem not to consider the love of Christ as a motive (or, at least, not as the best and principal motive) for obedience to his commands; but *content* themselves with dwelling on the rewards and punishments of the next world, and on the folly and danger of sin.

Such persons are undoubtedly right as far as they go; but they do not go far enough: the motives which they urge are not the only, nor the best, motives (though certainly very right and very powerful ones) for the practice of Christian duty. It is true, indeed, that *one* of the great purposes for which Christ came into the world, was to reveal to men the certainty of a future state of reward and punishment; and we find Him urging, briefly indeed, but forcibly, the immense importance of our eternal salvation above all worldly goods—the inconceivable happiness of good men hereafter, and the hopeless misery which awaits the disobedient: "What shall it profit a man, if he shall gain the whole world, and lose his own soul? Or what shall a man give in exchange for his soul?" He encourages us to despise worldly sufferings for righteousness' sake, by saying, "great is your reward in heaven;" and warns us to beware of displeasing that Being, "who hath power to destroy both soul and body in hell." And his followers hold the same language; they exhort their hearers to strive for "an incorruptible crown;" they tell them, that "the sufferings of this present time are not worthy to be compared with the glory that shall be revealed in us:" and, on the other hand, they profess, that, "knowing the terrors of the Lord, they teach men." Yet still it is to be observed, that this language of promise and threatening—this appeal to the *reason* and to the interests of men—is not the prevailing character—not the general tone, as it were —of the discourses of Christ and his apostles: at least, not when they are addressing *believers* in Christ. To those indeed who had any *doubts* of the nature of Christ's mission, or of the reality of the resurrection, they insisted much (as was manifestly necessary) on the certainty, and on the immense importance, of that future life, which our Lord had revealed: but when they were addressing their own disciples, who were familiar with those first rudiments of Christianity, to them, they chiefly insisted on *love* towards Christ, not certainly as a *substitute* for obedience, but as the great principle on which his followers ought to act— the main-spring of all their conduct. The misery of the bad, and the happiness of the good, hereafter, they all along presuppose and take for granted; but they seem to have regarded these doctrines as the foundation, not the completion—the beginning, not the end—of their system; to the further-advanced and better-instructed Christian, they held out a nobler and purer motive. " If ye love me," says our

Lord, "keep my commandments." "The love of Christ constraineth us," saith St. Paul; and he adds, as a reason, " that He died for all, that they which live, should not henceforth live unto themselves, but unto Him which died for them, and rose again[b]." And St. John, both in his Epistle and his Gospel, the latter of which, at least, may be supposed, from the lateness of its date, to have been more particularly addressed to those who were settled in the Christian faith, exhibits the same characteristics in a still more striking manner. In short, almost all the exhortations of the sacred writers are grounded on the infinite mercies of our great Instructor and Redeemer towards us, and on the gratitude, love, and reverence, which we ought to feel towards Him in return. To our hopes and fears, indeed, they appeal incidentally and occasionally; but the sentiment which they are continually striving to excite and keep alive in us, and which is the main-spring of their whole moral system, is, a strong sense of the greatness and the goodness

[b] 2 Cor. v. 14.

of our Saviour, and a fervent zeal in adoring and serving Him, who did and suffered so much for us.

To prove and illustrate what has now been affirmed, as fully as might be done, would be to transcribe the greater part of the apostolic epistles: the more any one examines them, the more he will perceive that their general tone and character is such as have been described.

Now let any one compare such language as this with the ideas which some Christian writers seem to entertain, and the language they use, and he will perceive, that, though undeniably just and right, they are very imperfect, and very far from resembling the model of Scripture. Such men are contented with the considerations that life is short, and death certain;—that all men must hereafter be judged before an all-seeing God, who will not fail to reward the good, and punish the bad;—that the greatest worldly goods and evils are mere trifles in comparison of our eternal happiness or misery; and that therefore it is the height of folly to be negligent in the performance of

our duty, or in avoiding temptations to sin,
since these are the points which most deserve
our attention, if we have any rational regard
for our own welfare. Nothing can be more
true than all this; and Christians are intended,
no doubt, most seriously to take it to heart,
and act constantly in conformity with such
principles; but still these, as has been said, are
not the only nor the highest principles on
which a Christian should act: these arguments
are what every Christian teacher ought to employ, but to which he should not confine himself: at least, if he would imitate the tone of
the Gospel. These topics indeed being almost
entirely drawn from what is commonly called
" natural religion," (as far at least as that is
supposed to hold out any probability of a
future state,) it follows of course, that to dwell
exclusively on these, is to omit great part of
what is peculiar to Christianity; and thus to
lose sight of one very striking and characteristic feature of it; a feature constituting one of
those peculiarities, the neglect or depreciation
of which is so common, and so carefully to be
guarded against.

Human ethics and natural religion may be sufficient to satisfy the understanding as to the nature and the claims of virtue; but to engage the feelings on the same side, belongs in an especial manner to the Gospel. It is necessary indeed to convince men's reason, and to point out to them their true interest; but Christ and his followers were not satisfied with this; they knew that it is in vain the reason is convinced, if the heart be not warmed; and that man will not follow his own interests, if all his affections lie the other way. That this should be the case with rational beings, is the great paradox which we in vain endeavour to explain, though daily experience compels us to acknowledge it; and to find a remedy for this weakness—to induce men to pursue the line of conduct which their own sober judgment admits to be the best—has been attempted by all moralists; though not very successfully, and not always judiciously. Our Lord and his followers, who "knew what was in man," were well aware that such a Being could not be practically influenced by an appeal to his understanding alone. They did not therefore make religion a matter of mere prudent calculation, but of affectionate zeal. When Christ was committing to Simon Peter the care of the beloved flock which He had himself redeemed, He meant him indeed to understand, no doubt, that he would be punished if he neglected this charge, and that great would be the reward of diligent obedience; but these were not the topics He chose to insist upon: "Simon son of Jonas, lovest thou me?" Peter replied, "Lord, thou knowest that I love thee;" Jesus said unto him, "Feed my sheep." Thrice was this injunction given, and thrice was the appeal made, not to the hopes and fears, but to the *affections,* of the apostle.

In like manner, St. Paul, in exhorting the Churches, alludes *occasionally* only to the rewards and punishments of a future state, and the folly of not preparing for it; but he insists *continually* on the mercies which God has *already* shewn us, and the gratitude we ought to feel for them, and strives to fill us with an earnest desire of pleasing Him, and an abhorrence of sin, as odious in his sight. For example, when he tells the Colossians "to forgive one another, if any man have a quarrel against any," it is on this ground, "even as Christ forgave you:" and again, "Children, obey your parents in all things, for this is *well-pleasing unto the Lord.*" And again, "Be ye followers of God as *dear children*; and walk in love, as Christ also hath *loved us*, and hath *given himself* for us."

From these and innumerable similar passages it is sufficiently evident, that the Christian, if he would listen to and imitate the teaching of Christ and his apostles, must not be contented to dwell merely on the rewards and punishments of the next world, and the importance of striving for the one, and guarding against the other, (though these should be ever present to his mind;) but he must also endeavour to "set his *affection* on things above;—to fill his heart with the love of Christ— with admiration for the blended majesty and loveliness displayed in his sojourning on earth —with gratitude, not only for the redemption by Him, but also for his condescending goodness in visiting his people in the flesh, to declare to them the invisible God—and with an active zeal to serve Him as perfectly as possible, in *proof* of his reverence and affection. These are the prevailing and principal motives in the mind of a sincere Christian: these are what our Lord and his followers were the most anxious to instil into the hearts of their disciples.

The views (again) which the sacred writers give of the rewards prepared for the faithful in the next life, (dim and imperfect as they are,) correspond in the most natural and striking manner with their mode of inculcating Christian duty; and those whose topics of exhortation on this latter point are exclusively addressed to the head, and not to the heart, labour under a corresponding defect in their manner of speaking of future happiness; their views of which, accordingly, are, as well as their moral precepts, needlessly dry, unattractive, and uninteresting to the feelings. They keep out of sight, throughout, the *personal* character of our religion, and of every thing connected with it: i. e. its continual reference to *persons*, and especially to that Great Person who is the Author of it, rather than to mere abstract *things*. While they dwell, in delineating and enforcing duty, exclusively on the excellence and advantage of a virtuous life—of obeying the dictates of a well-regulated conscience—of walking in the path of moral rectitude, and the like—they speak also in a corresponding tone of the infinite value of an eternity of happiness; of being freed from the evils and imperfections of our present state; of escaping the horrors of endless remorse; and of being exalted into a new and superior condition; with much of the same kind, that is perfectly true indeed, and deserving of being kept in mind, but which is far less *interesting* (when such topics are dwelt on exclusively) than the continual reference to *persons,* which we find in the sacred writers.

As St. Paul's favourite exhortations (if I may so speak) to personal holiness, whether he is directing our views to future reward, or to the other incentive just mentioned, consist in a reference, of some sort or other, to Jesus Christ; so, his allusions to that reward itself are of a corresponding character. In the inculcation of virtue he dwells, as has been just remarked, on the example Jesus left us, that " we should walk in his steps ;" he speaks of " walking in love, as Christ also hath loved us ;"—of " putting on Christ ;"—of being " buried *with Him* in baptism;"—of being " risen with Christ;"—of doing " what is well-pleasing to the Lord Jesus Christ;" —of our being " followers of him (Paul) even as he is of Christ ;" and the like : not speaking so often of *Christian virtue* in the abstract, as he does of it embodied, as it were, exemplified, represented, *personified,* in Jesus Christ; " *looking unto Jesus,* the Author and Finisher of our faith," at every step. And his language in speaking of the Christian's *hopes,* corresponds with that concerning Christian *duties :* he does not speak so much of eternal happiness *in the abstract,* as of the happiness of an intimate union with our great Master; to die is, with him, " to depart and *to be with Christ ;*" after " having suffered with Him, to reign also *with Him;*" of " the crown of glory, which He, the righteous Lord, has prepared for all that *love his appearing:*" and his encouragement to the Colossians is, " so shall we ever be *with the Lord."* Thus also St. John (as well befitted the beloved disciple) places both all Christian perfection in conformity to the pattern, and all happiness and glory in admission to the presence, of our great Master: " we know not what we shall be; but we know, that, when He shall appear, we shall be like Him, for we shall see Him as He is." And our Lord's own language is of the same tone: as the motive He seeks to implant in the disciples' breast is, as has been said, love, gratitude, and reverence for Himself, so the encouragement He sets before them is the hope not merely of happiness in the abstract, but of intimate union and close intercourse with Himself: " If ye love me, keep my commandments." " If a man love me he will keep my saying, and my Father will love him, and *we will come unto him, and make our abode with him."* " I will not leave you comfortless; I will *come unto you."* " That *where I am,* there ye may be also," &c.

All this is admirably suited both to what man *is,* and to what he *ought* to be: as emulation is a natural principle, and a good example accordingly more instructive and more impressive than the best general maxims, so, the thought, whom we are *to live with*—for what sort of *society* we are to fit ourselves, affects the mind much more strongly than any general description of what that life itself shall be. That the chief part of the happiness therefore which is prepared for the faithful in a better world is to consist in a more perfect knowledge of our Redeemer, and closer intercourse with Him, serves on the one hand to interest, and encourage, and delight the right minded Christian, and to admonish, and warn, and improve, one who is not such. This world being, as we are taught, not merely a state of *trial*, but also of *preparation*, no precepts can be so advantageous to us with this view, as to be told what sort of society it is *for which* we are required to prepare ourselves. No general rules, however copious and precise, can equal the combined effect of the example of a particular *person* set before us, together with a notice that for his society we are required to endeavour to qualify ourselves. And accordingly St. John adds, immediately after the passage just cited, " Every one that hath *this hope* in Him, purifieth himself even *as He is pure.*"

This mode of moral training, adopted by Christ and his Apostles, is among those peculiarities of the Gospel system which most demand our admiration. The motives which they inculcated, were both the most effectual, and also the most pure and elevated; their plan of endeavouring to win over the affections, to gain the hearts, of their converts, was not only the most likely to make men perform their duty, but also made that duty itself more acceptable.

If it be possible for any one to become what is commonly called a good moral man, wholly and solely from perceiving that it is his *interest* to be so, because he will be rewarded if he does right, and punished if he does wrong, still his service will not only be very cold and heartless, but also very deficient; he will be wanting in alacrity of duty—in abhorrence of sin—in love for his best friend—in gratitude towards his highest benefactor. No one would much prize a friend (or rather he would be reckoned unworthy of the name) who felt no regard for him, but did him service merely because he perceived it was for his own interest, and that he should be a sufferer if he neglected him. Neither will Christ accept this kind of service from his followers. He requires them to give up their hearts to Him, and to obey Him, not merely as servants, but as affectionate children. None of their duties, though ever so well performed, are pleasing in his sight, unless they proceed from a love, reverence, and gratitude towards Him, similar to that which we feel for a most excellent parent. " Ye are my friends," says He, " if ye do whatsoever I command you ; henceforth I call you not servants,—but I have called you friends." And again, " Whosoever shall do the will of God, the same is my brother, and my sister, and mother[c]." In reality, however, it is hardly possible, that a man *can* be virtuous in other respects who is destitute of these feelings. Many objects there are in this world which will always engage our affections very

[c] May not this expression of our Lord's, and also another, (Luke xi. 28.) have been intended partly a warning against the Romish error, of deifying (as it may fairly be called) the Virgin Mary?

strongly : if then *none* of our *feelings* are engaged on the side of our religious duties—no part of our affections fixed on our Redeemer— can it be expected, that calm reasoning and cool calculation will alone be sufficient to keep us steady and active in our duty, in opposition to so many lively emotions, in preference to so many tempting objects ? No prudent man will trust to such a plan in the education of youth : men are not satisfied with pointing out to a young person the necessity of being diligent in his business, inasmuch as on that depends his subsistence, and all his hopes of wealth and distinction ; but they strive also to inspire him with a *love* for his employment—a *taste* for his profession, whatever it may be ; they know that sentiments of this kind will be his best safeguard against the many temptations to indolence and dissipation. Surely the path of Christian duty is not beset with *fewer* temptations; nor is it *less* necessary, in this far greater concern, to engage the feelings on the right side.

Christ and his apostles knew human nature too well not to perceive this ; when therefore they had convinced the reason of men, their next endeavour was to mend their hearts; those warm affections which God has implanted in our breasts, and which were never meant to be rooted out, *they* strove to fix on the most suitable and the noblest objects; well aware, that when this is accomplished, men will not merely know their duty, but practise it with zeal, and spirit, and pleasure. They well knew, that a cold address to the understanding—a mere chain of arguments—serves rather to teach men what they ought to do, than to excite them actually to do it; it may lead them to *think* rightly about religion, but not to *feel* and *act* rightly: it is like the moon light, clear indeed and beautiful, but powerless and cold; *their* preaching, on the contrary, was like the light of the sun, which warms while it illuminates, and not only adorns, but fertilizes the earth. For it must never be forgotten, (as, indeed, has been already observed,) that it is in vain the affections are excited, if the practice is not improved; it is in vain that the artificer heats and melts his metal, if he neglects to mould it into the proper form. Indeed, those who do not live a Christian life, may, from that very circumstance, be assured, that they *have not true, genuine,* and *steady* Christian feelings. Sudden and short bursts of devout fervor will not produce a uniform, careful, and active course of virtue; but a rational and deep-fixed love of God undoubtedly will. A man may deceive both others and himself by extravagant language and enthusiastic emotions, which may pass for proofs of extraordinary holiness; but he cannot so deceive Christ; who has sufficiently taught us, that He will expect good conduct as the *fruit* of good sentiments—the keeping of his commandments as the *proof* of our loving Him sincerely. No man, indeed, would ever be deceived in any other similar case; he would well know how to estimate the pretended affection of one, who should profess the warmest regard for him, yet pay no attention to his wishes, and use no exertions in his service, but *act* rather like an *enemy* than a friend. And as such a person would be regarded by men, so will those be in the sight of God, who profess to love Him, and yet neglect to obey Him.

To the above considerations it should be

added, that the Christian's "reasonable service," grounded on such motives, is not only
more perfect, and also more acceptable, than
any others could produce, but likewise (when
the habit is in some degree formed) incomparably less burdensome, and more pleasing. Indeed, even in the affairs of this world, the
affectionate parent, child, husband, wife, and
friend, know by experience how greatly *Love*
lightens every task : and those who will " come
unto Christ," with such feelings as He merits
and demands, will find experimentally, that
" his yoke is easy, and his burden light :" they
will " find rest unto their souls," if, in answer
to that question, which He asks alike of all his
followers, " Lovest thou me?" they can answer, with sincerity and truth, " Lord, thou
knowest that I love thee."

If the view which has been here taken of
this subject be correct, it follows, that Christianity stands distinguished from all systems
of religion, or of philosophy, which unaided
reason can devise, no less by the motives to
which it appeals—the frame of mind from which
it requires moral conduct to spring—than by

those other peculiarities formerly mentioned. For a rational and firm assurance of a future resurrection to immortality, we must resort to the Gospel;—for the hopes of eternal happiness, we must look to Him, who has not only announced but purchased it:—for such a manifestation of the Godhead as may excite us to affectionate piety, and for such a model of human virtue as may be securely imitated, we shall vainly seek, except in the Gospel; and it is there also, and there alone, that we find morality inculcated, not only on the ground of those promises and threatenings which it sets before us, but also of those affections which it is so remarkably and peculiarly calculated to excite. If mere external acts of duty were all that is required, this kind of precept would still be far superior to a mere appeal to men's reason, and would produce a larger amount of good conduct; much greater then will its superiority appear, when we consider how much nobler and more intrinsically valuable is that good conduct which springs from a pious, and grateful, and affectionate heart.

Let no one then lose sight of, nor under-

value, these admirable, these divine peculiarities of our religion, which furnish the only
effectual means of counteracting the weakness
of man's nature. Let no one, under pretence
of laying a firm foundation of Natural Religion,
render the superstructure of Christianity insignificant, by attributing to natural religion what
revelation alone can furnish: and, above all,
let us not—carelessly blind to those splendid
characteristics which distinguish it—confound
this religion with the various systems of philosophical speculation, or of popular superstition, which have successively occupied mankind; but keep our eyes stedfastly fixed, as
it were, on the star which stands over the holy
Infant at Bethlehem, and which has no fellow
in the firmament.

But though enough is revealed to us in
Scripture to instruct us in our duty, and to
incite us to the practice of it, there is much
also that is *not* revealed, which many, at least,
would be eagerly desirous to know: it sup-
presses much of what some vainly seek to find
in it, or complain of not finding; which all
pretended revelations profess, and might be

expected to profess, to make known; and which a true revelation, and none but a true one, might be expected to omit. The peculiarity in our religion, which is here alluded to, will form the subject of the next Essay.

ESSAY IV.

ON THE PRACTICAL CHARACTER OF REVELATION.

WHEN Moses tells the Israelites, that "the secret things belong unto the Lord our God; but those things which are revealed belong unto us and to our children for ever, that we may do all the words of this law," he plainly implies, not only that of the designs and attributes of the Almighty there are some which He has vouchsafed to make known to mankind by revelation, and others which He has thought fit to keep secret; but also, that those which *are* revealed, have a reference to human conduct, and are, in some way or other, of a practical nature. Such at least is declared to be the character of that revelation which was made to the Israelites.

Now since it is undeniable that there have been, and are, many systems of false religion

in the world, all of which profess to reveal
something as to the nature of God, and his
dealings with his creatures, this circumstance
is frequently dwelt upon by those who studiously endeavour to confound all religions together, with a view to hold up all to equal
contempt, as so many various systems of imposture and delusion: and others again,
though they do not absolutely reject our religion, are yet so far misled by this fallacy, as
to regard it with indifference. It will be worth
while therefore to examine attentively the point
above mentioned ; I mean, the exclusively *practical* character which Moses appears to attribute to his revelation ; and to enquire, whether it is likely to constitute an important and
distinguishing feature in any professed revelation which may possess it : in other words,
whether the abstaining from *points of mere
curiosity*, be a probable *mark of a true revelation.*

This enquiry falls naturally under two heads ;
first, whether or not a *pretended* revelation is
likely to contain any matters which are interesting to curiosity alone, and have no re-

ference to practice; and secondly, whether this is likely to be the case with a *true* revelation.

The former of these questions we need not hesitate, I think, to answer in the affirmative.

That the desire of knowledge, for its own sake, is a part of our nature, is a truth so obvious, as hardly to need being insisted on. For though it is common to hear men imply the contrary, by asking contemptuously, in the case of some pursuit for which they happen to have no relish, "What is the use of learning this or that? What advantage is to be derived from such and such a branch of knowledge?" yet the very same persons, if some discovery be the next moment announced to them, of a different kind, which may happen to fall in with their own taste, will probably be found to manifest the liveliest interest, and the most eager curiosity, even where they would be at a loss to point out what practical advantage they are likely to derive from it. So far indeed is utility from being the sole standard of value in men's minds, that even such knowledge as *is* useful, is in general sought more for its own sake, than with a view to utility; nor are men ever more eager in the pursuit of it, than when they have no further object to occupy them: "accordingly," as is justly observed by an ancient writer, who well understood human nature, "when we are at leisure from the cares of necessary business, then are we eager to see, to hear, to learn, something; regarding the knowledge of what is hidden, or of what is admirable, as an essential ingredient of happiness[d]." He is quite right in the circumstances fixed on as most exciting our interest; things *hidden*, and things *admirable*, being what men especially covet to know. Now nothing can be more hidden, nothing more admirable, than the nature, and the works, of God. The origin and constitution of the world we inhabit—of the rest of that vast system of which it forms a part—and of man himself—the nature of various orders of Beings, which may exist, superior to man, and of the Supreme Being himself—each of these subjects suggests innumerable matters of enquiry, whose grandeur fills the most exalted, and whose difficulty

---

[d] Cicero de Officiis, b. 1.

baffles the most intelligent, mind. Is it not then natural, that men should eagerly seek for some superhuman means of information on subjects so interesting to their curiosity, and so much beyond their unaided powers? And is it not consequently to be expected, that both the devices of an impostor, and the visions of an enthusiast, should abound in food for this curiosity?—that the one should seek for proselytes by professing to communicate what men are so desirous of knowing; and that the other should be altogether occupied with those questions to which the imagination of men is so naturally turned, till a diseased fancy mistakes its day-dreams for a revelation?

Such, I say, is what we might be prepared, from the nature of man, to expect: and if we consult history we shall find our conjecture fully borne out by facts. In all those other religions, and in all those modifications of our own, which we attribute to the imagination or to the artifice of man, the pretended revelations not only abound with matters of speculative curiosity unconnected with practice, but are sometimes even principally made up of them, so as to appear to have for their chief object the communication of knowledge concerning heavenly things, for its own sake. To illustrate this by a full examination of all the various systems of false revelation, would be manifestly both tedious and unnecessary: tedious, inasmuch as even a brief sketch of them would occupy a considerable volume; and unnecessary, for most readers, since a few moments' recollection will enable them to recall from their previous knowledge enough to confirm, to a great degree at least, the remark which has just been made: and the conclusion will be the more strengthened, the further the enquiry is pursued. Let any one consider, for instance, the Greek and Roman mythology: what is the character of that infinite number of fables, delivered by pretenders either to immediate inspiration, or to traditional knowledge of revelation, respecting the genealogies of their deities, their transformations, their contests, their adventures on earth? Our present business is not with the absurdity of these fables, nor with their immoral tendency, nor their want of evidence, nor the degree of credit they obtained;

let our attention be confined to the single circumstance of their general want of *reference to
human conduct*—their being principally calculated to attract and amuse an inquisitive mind.
It is true, indeed, that direct practical precepts
and examples do form some part of the Pagan
religions; but by no means the greatest or most
prominent part; and it is speaking far within
compass to say, that most of what the ancients
were taught respecting their gods, could not even
be imagined to be of any practical importance,
but related merely to the gratification of curiosity.

If we examine the pretended revelations of
the Hindoos and of other modern Pagans, we
find the very same principle exhibited in other
forms: the names and the achievements of
their gods are different, but the general character is the same; the leading object, or, at least,
one leading object, in both, is to gratify men's
curiosity about the nature and the operations
of superior agents—about the state of things
in another world.

If we turn from these apocryphal and
undigested heaps of fabulous tradition,
to the more systematic imposture of

Mahomet, a man doubtless of no mean ability,—who had the advantage of borrowing from Judaism and from Christianity whatever might suit his purpose, and who certainly understood, as experience has proved, the art of alluring converts,—we shall find our expectations as to the point in question still confirmed. Not that the Koran is wanting in moral precept and exhortation ; for it abounds in them to the most tedious minuteness of detail; but it also abounds with the most elaborate descriptions of heaven and its inhabitants, and of other (pretended) works of God ; with full and circumstantial narratives of the creation of the world, and of various other transactions, ascribed to the Deity, all calculated to gratify the prying—one might even say, the impertinent —curiosity of man respecting divine mysteries ; but so utterly unconnected with human duties, that the mere increase of knowledge, for its own sake, as an ultimate end, is made to appear one principal object of this pretended revelation.

It would be wearisome and disgusting to introduce such specimens as would fully illustrate what has been asserted; though it is scarcely possible adequately to describe in words how forcibly it will be impressed on the mind, on actual perusal, that the prevailing character of the book in question is such as has been described. But those who will be at the pains to examine this and other pretended revelations, with an express view to the subject of our present enquiry, will meet with abundant instances to confirm what has been here advanced; more than they perhaps are aware of, if they have a general acquaintance with those systems, but have never considered them with reference to the particular point now before us. Such an enquiry, it may be safely affirmed, would be profitable and satisfactory, if fully pursued; and would communicate a lively interest to the perusal even of the most absurd reveries of heathen mythology, and of the Koran: but it will be sufficient in this place to have suggested some of the principal points towards which the enquiry should be directed.

In addition to those pretended revelations which have been the basis of distinct religions, we should also turn our attention to those which have been connected with modifications of our own. Not to dwell on the fables of the Jewish Talmud, which may fairly be placed under this head, and which will be found to correspond with the principle originally laid down,—thus proving, among other things, that the Jewish nation had, of themselves, in an eminent degree, the same taste in respect of these matters as the Gentiles,—what a multitude of idle legends do we meet with in the Romish Church, that have no more reference to practice than the heathen mythology! I speak not now of the extravagance and impiety of many of them; nor of the *too great* reference to conduct of some others, whose tendency is to recommend a life of useless seclusion, or of superstitious self-torture, in preference to active virtue: but a large portion of them have no conceivable reference to conduct whatever, and are fitted merely to amuse the roving imagination, and gratify the presumptuous curiosity of the credulous.

Lastly, to advert to a more recent instance, look to the visions of the pretended prophet Swedenborg; himself the dupe, as is generally supposed, of his own distempered fancy. It is well known, that he professed to have been favoured with most copious and distinct revelations—to have visited the celestial abodes, and to have conversed with various orders of Beings; of all which he gives minute descriptions: yet though his followers insist much on the importance of believing in this pretended revelation, it would, I believe, be difficult for them to state even any one point in which a man is called upon to alter either his conduct, his motives, or his moral sentiments, in consequence of such belief. The system furnishes abundant matter of faith, and food for curiosity; but has little or no intelligible reference to practice.

Such then being the character of false religions, what may we expect from a true one? Since both reason and experience shew, that it is the obvious policy of an impostor, and the most natural delusion of a visionary, to treat much of curious and hidden matters, relative to the divine operations, beyond what is conducive to practical instruction, it should next be considered whether the case is likely to be

the same with a real revelation; whether *that*
also is likely to be much occupied in minister-
ing to speculative curiosity. Now this question we may on good grounds answer in the
negative: for the *general* rule of Providence
evidently is, that man should be left to supply
his own wants, and seek knowledge, both practical and speculative, by the aid of those faculties which have been originally bestowed on
him; a revelation is an extraordinary and
miraculous *exception* to this general rule; and
it seems therefore reasonable to conclude, that
it should be bestowed for some very important
purpose. Now the knowledge of our duty, beyond what is discoverable by unaided reason—
instruction how we are to serve God, and
obtain his favour—does seem a sufficiently important purpose; but not so, the mere gratification of curiosity. The desire of knowledge
is indeed implanted in us by our Creator; and
the pursuit of it is an innocent, and honourable,
and highly pleasurable employment of our
faculties: but there is a sufficiently wide field
of investigation within the reach of our natural
faculties; there seems no reason why the Al-

mighty should work a miracle for the increase of our mere speculative knowledge: not to mention that our gratification consists more in the *pursuit* and *acquirement*, by our own efforts, of such knowledge, than in the *possession* of it. Whatever therefore it concerns us practically to know, with a view to the regulation of the heart and conduct—whatever God requires us to be, and to do, in order to become acceptable in his sight—this, it seems consonant to his justice and goodness to declare to us by revelation, when of ourselves we are incompetent to discover it; but that He should miraculously reveal any thing besides this, for the gratification of an inquisitive mind, there seems no good reason to expect.

It may be said indeed, that the trial of our faith, humility, and candour, in assenting, on sufficient authority, to mysterious doctrines, is a worthy and fit purpose, for which such doctrines may be revealed: this is undoubtedly true; and the purpose may even be fairly reckoned a practical one, since so good a moral effect results from such belief. If therefore none of the doctrines necessary to be revealed for *other* practical purposes were of such a mysterious character as to serve for trials of faith also, we might perhaps expect that some things should be proposed to our belief, solely and singly for this latter purpose. But if both objects can be fully accomplished by the same revelation—if our faith be sufficiently tried by the admission of such mysterious doctrines as are important for other practical ends also—then the revelation of any further mysteries, which lead to no such practical end, is the less necessary, and consequently the less to be expected.

What then is in this respect the character of our religion? It may safely be asserted that it is precisely such as, we have seen, a true revelation might be expected to be: that it teaches us what is needful for us to know, but little or nothing besides; that the information it imparts is such as concerns the regulation of our character and practice, but leaves our curiosity unsatisfied.

Those who are sufficiently conversant with the Scriptures, will at once recognize this as a characteristic feature of them: to prove the point in question as fully as might be done, would require a detailed examination of the whole Bible : and such an examination diligently conducted with a view to the particular point before us, is one which may be recommended not merely to professed theological students, but (since it calls for no great ingenuity or learning) to Christian readers in general; as neither an unprofitable nor unpleasing enquiry, to him who delights in contrasting the wisdom and the dignified simplicity of God's word, with the idle and arrogant pretensions of human fraud and folly.

The generally practical tendency of the Scripture revelations, and their omission of every thing that would serve merely to pamper vain curiosity, will not fail to strike any candid reader in the course of such an examination. It will be sufficient in this place to suggest a few hints respecting the principles on which this enquiry should be conducted.

I. In the first place we should bear in mind what parts of the Bible are to be regarded as strictly and properly bearing the character of *Revelation.* The greater part of it is historical;

and though we believe the sacred historians to have been under the guidance of the Holy Spirit to lead them into all necessary truth—to guard them against any material error—and, in some few cases, to inform them of what could not be known by human means—yet the very nature of history is such, that it would be unreasonable to expect to find each single event that is narrated to be a matter of high importance: the age and name, for example, of any one Jewish king, as it is not, so far as we can see, a point of itself necessary to be known as essential to our religion, so neither is it properly a point of miraculous revelation; it is a part of the *history*; and if that history, *taken collectively*, be, as it is, highly instructive, and illustrative of those divine dispensations in which we are concerned, it must be allowed to possess sufficiently that practical character which we are authorized to expect.

As for those parts which necessarily imply a supernatural communication made to the writer, such as, for example, the account of the creation of the world, nothing is more striking than their uncircumstantial brevity, which leaves the curiosity of the reader altogether unsatisfied. This circumstance has indeed been sometimes complained of, and even, with a strange perversity, urged as an objection against Scripture, on the ground that an inspired writer must have had it in his *power* to satisfy them as to the detail of these interesting events; and that consequently it was to be expected of him. Now had Moses been an impostor, undoubtedly he would, with such a knowledge of human nature as he plainly manifests, have obviated this objection (as Mahomet has done) by inventing abundance of circumstances; but for a *true* revelation to forestall the discoveries of astronomy and geology, was neither necessary nor proper: being no part of religion, they are altogether foreign from the purposes of revelation. It is indeed of the highest importance in a religious point of view, to be assured that the earth, with its various races of inhabitants, together with the rest of the universe, are neither eternal, nor the work of chance, or of any non-intelligent agent, nor of *various* creative powers; but that One God is the Author of all: thus much accordingly is clearly revealed: but innumerable circumstances, which it does not concern us to know, though they strongly interest our curiosity, are suppressed. Now this, we contend, is a mark of a true revelation; since in that, and in that alone, it is to be expected.

The complaint has indeed been urged, that not only the true account of physical phenomena has been suppressed, but also that wrong notions respecting them have been conveyed. But he who can seriously object to the want of philosophical correctness in such passages, for example, as those which speak of the rising and setting of the sun, should recollect, that when occasion called for an allusion to such matters, unless language conformable to the popular ideas had been employed, one of two alternatives must have been adopted; either men must have been fully instructed by revelation in the Newtonian system, or they must have been addressed in a style which, though in itself correct, would have been to them utterly unintelligible: whether either of these modes of procedure would have been better suited to the object of a revelation than the one adopted, we may leave the objector to determine. But if we compare, as to this point, the Bible with the pretended revelation of Mahomet, we shall be struck with the contrast : for *he* goes out of his way, as it were, to assert *gratuitously*, and with distinct particularity, many points of the astronomical theory which prevailed in his time; and thus expressly commits himself as to the truth of an erroneous system[e].

II. Another circumstance to be kept in view in the proposed examination is, that when we may be at a loss to understand the *ultimate* purpose of any part of our revelation, still, if we perceive an *immediate* purpose that is practical, we must be careful not to confound this case with that of a supposed revelation which has no perceptible purpose at all : if, in short, it be plain, that something is to be done in consequence of what is revealed, even though we may not understand why that particular duty *should* be enjoined, still the revelation is evidently practical; and is therefore conform-

[e] As, for instance, where he speaks of the east and west as *determinate points* in the globe, in the same manner as the north and south poles are.

able to the principle above laid down. For example, nothing can be more evidently practical than the whole of what was revealed to Moses respecting the Jewish ritual : for though we may not understand for what reasons the Jews were commanded to perform such and such ceremonies, yet that there was something to be *performed*, is undeniable.

III. Lastly, we should consider, that some parts of revelation may have a practical importance relative to some particular times, persons, and circumstances, but not to all. For example, many of the prophetic visions and declarations pertaining to the kingdom of the Messiah, must have been very obscure as to their true purport, till they were cleared up by his advent ; but *then* they furnished both a proof and an explanation of his religion. In like manner also, many similar prophecies, both in the Old and New Testament, may be designed to answer the same purpose hereafter, when the appointed period shall arrive, which is to bring with it at once their fulfilment, their explanation, and their practical use. Others, on the contrary, which are now among the most obscure, may have been both intelligible and edifying to many of the contemporaries of the prophets themselves, for whose use they may have been (as in many instances we plainly see they were) principally designed.

But it is very observable, that in most of those cases where we are least able to perceive the practical advantage of the revelation given, the very obscurity and indistinctness which are complained of serve as a confirmation of the point maintained : for these obscure passages *excite* curiosity indeed, but do not *gratify* it : the very objection which some bring against them is, not that too much is revealed, with a view to speculative knowledge, but that too little is revealed. Now with a false revelation the case is exactly reversed ; for that will always abound with copious and distinct, though unprofitable, descriptions of whatever is marvellous, and calculated to strike the imagination, and to amuse an inquisitive mind.

Keeping in mind the considerations which have been here offered, we shall find on examination of the Scriptures, that it is a characteristic of the revelation they contain, to withhold such knowledge as is merely speculative —to leave abstract curiosity unsatisfied—and to inform us of little or nothing except what it concerns us for some practical purpose to know.

Nothing could have been more interesting to man's curiosity, than a full account of a future state; and accordingly the Koran abounds with the most copious and high-wrought descriptions of paradise and hell, and of the details of the day of judgment. The writers of our Scriptures, on the contrary, while they are perpetually enforcing with all earnestness the reality of this future state, so important in practice, strictly confine themselves to the most general and brief description of it. Again, the principles on which different classes of mankind will be judged, and the future fate of those who never heard of revelation, are a highly interesting subject of enquiry, but one from which Scripture carefully abstains, except so far as is needful for us to know: "Strive to enter in at the straight gate," is our Lord's answer to those who enquired as to the number of the saved; and He scarcely adverts at all to the case of the unenlightened, except to inculcate the heavier responsibility of those who sin against revealed knowledge, above those who offended merely against the light of natural reason: "The servant who knew his Lord's will, and did it not, shall be beaten with many stripes." All this, as might be expected, is exactly reversed in the Koran, which describes at large the final condemnation of all mankind except Mahometans; and of these, such as are punished for their sins, so far from being judged more guilty, as having sinned against better knowledge, are described as finally to be restored, by their belief in the prophet, and received into paradise. Such certainly is the revelation, and such the doctrine, which a false teacher would naturally deliver.

There are, however, some things, I am well aware, revealed in the Gospel, which but too many, even of those who assent to them, are inclined to consider as mere speculative articles of faith: as, for example, the revelation of God to us, not merely as our Creator and Governor, but also as our incarnate Redeemer, and as the Holy Ghost our Sanctifier. But we may safely affirm, that whoever does not perceive in these doctrines any practical tendency, (including in that expression, as we certainly ought, whatever has a reference to the affections and motives, as well as to mere external conduct,) has not yet gained a just and adequate notion of what the Christian religion is.

Fully to refute such an error, would be to give a complete explanation of the whole system of the Gospel: let it suffice, therefore, to make an *appeal* to Scripture, and to refer thither both the infidel and the believer, who deny the practical tendency of any of its doctrines, that they may understand what the Gospel really is; the one, before he too hastily rejects it, and the other, before he too hastily builds his hopes on it. A careful and candid perusal of the Bible will sufficiently evince, that, at least, the sacred writers themselves were very far from conceiving that the doctrines they delivered were mere speculative matters of faith, unconnected with any change in the heart and conduct. If they inform us, that " the grace of God, which bringeth salvation,

hath appeared unto men," it is " to teach us,
that, denying ungodliness and worldly lusts,
we should live soberly, righteously, and godly
in this present world;" when they describe to
us "God manifest in the flesh," they instruct
us to look to Him with devout trust, and to
shape our lives after the model of his perfection: " Let this mind be in you, which was
also in Christ Jesus :" when they " preach
Christ crucified," it is that we, while we " cru-
cify the old man with the affections and lusts,"
may yet with grateful humility renounce all
arrogant confidence in our own merits, and
look for salvation to his : and that while we
trust in the Divine mercy for the pardon of
sin, we may not attribute this pardon, purchased by such a sacrifice, to his lightly regarding sin, but may be sensible of its deadly
nature, and its odiousness in God's sight: when
they announce his resurrection, it is that we
may be exhorted to rise also from the death of
sin to a life of holiness, that, " being risen with
Christ, we may set our affection on things
above ;" and may be encouraged to look forward to a final victory over the grave: and

when the love of God towards us is set forth,
it is given as a reason why " we ought also to
love one another," and to testify our sense of
his goodness by keeping his commandments.

In short, as the doctrine of the Trinity may
be considered as containing a summary and
compendium of the Christian Faith, so, its
application may be regarded as a summary of
Christian practice; which may be said to be
comprised in this; that as we believe God to
stand in three relations *to us*, we also must
practically keep in view the three *corresponding
relations* in which, as is plainly implied by that
doctrine, we stand *towards Him;* as, first, the
creatures and " children of God ;" secondly, as
the " redeemed and purchased people " of Jesus
Christ ; and, thirdly, as " the temples of the
Holy Ghost" our Sanctifier.

On such topics, and with such views, the
sacred writers dwell with the utmost copiousness, distinctness, and earnestness ; but as to
the mere increase of speculative knowledge,
they are scanty, indistinct, and apparently indifferent. Take, as one instance out of many,
the allusion which St. Paul makes in the

twelfth chapter of his second Epistle to the
Corinthians, to the celestial vision with which
he had been favoured; nothing is said of it in
any other part of his writings; nor does it
appear whether he had even ever mentioned it
till then, though it had occurred fourteen years
before: he mentions it *then* for a practical purpose, viz. to impress the Corinthians (who
knew that his own report of a *fact* was to be
credited) with a due sense of his apostolic dignity and authority, which they had been disposed to depreciate: and he speaks with the
utmost possible brevity of his being " caught
up into paradise," and " hearing unspeakable
words," without relating any particulars of the
vision. It is truly edifying to compare this
with Mahomet's long and circumstantial description of his pretended visit to heaven, filled
with a multitude of needless particulars, calculated to gratify an appetite for the marvellous. That man must be a bad judge of the
characters of truth and falsehood, who can
peruse the two accounts without coming to the
conclusion, that the one bears the marks of
reality, as plainly as the other does of fiction;

and that the narrative of St. Paul, as well as his general tone, is as suitable to a true apostle, as that of Mahomet is, to an impostor.

There is another example, which deserves selection, as a very striking one, of the uncircumstantial and practical character of the Christian revelations: St. Peter, in his second Epistle, adverts to the deluge, and also to the final destruction of the earth: we may be sure his readers would have been much interested by a circumstantial description of both those events; and we may be nearly as sure, that had he been a false pretender to inspiration, he would have gratified their curiosity: as it is, however, he dispatches the subject in five or six verses, and in such terms as convey little or nothing more than the *certainty* of the event; and then proceeds at once to a practical conclusion: "Seeing then that all these things shall be dissolved, what manner of persons ought ye to be in all holy conversation and godliness."

St. Paul also, in speaking of the same subject, having told the Corinthians, that at the last day "we shall all be changed," and that

the blest shall be " clothed upon" with a body
" like unto the glorious body of Christ," proceeds, instead of detailing any of the circumstances of so interesting a change, or fully
describing the glorified body of " saints made
perfect," to exhort them to " be stedfast, and
abounding in the work of the Lord, since they
know that their labour is not in vain." Such
passages in the works of these apostles may
furnish the most unlearned Christian with " a
reason for the faith that is in him," consolatory
to his own mind, and unanswerable by infidels. He may ask them, how it came to pass,
that no one of our sacred writers has given a
full, minute, and engaging account of all that
is (according to him) to take place at the end
of the world ;—of all the interesting particulars
of the day of judgment ;—of the new bodies
with which men will arise ;—and of " the glories that shall be revealed" in heaven. It is
plain, that nothing could have been more *gratifying* to the curiosity of all who had an interest in the subject ; nothing more likely even
to *allure* fresh converts, than a glowing description of the joys of heaven ; it would have

been easily *believed* too, by those who gave credit to the writer, as it is plain St. Paul supposed the Corinthians did ;—it would have been very *easy* for an *impostor* to give a loose to his fancy, in inventing such a description ; and to an *enthusiast* it would have been unavoidable; he who was passing off his day-dreams for revelations, on himself, as well as on others, would have been sure to dream largely on such a subject. Why then did not St. Paul do any thing of the kind? I answer, because he was *not* an impostor, nor an enthusiast; but taught only what had been actually revealed to him, and what he was commanded to reveal to others. Let infidels give any other answer to the question if they can. They have had near two thousand years to try; and never yet have they been able to explain the dry, brief, uncircumstantial, unadorned, unpretending accounts which our sacred writers give, of things the most interesting to human curiosity, on any other supposition than that of their being honest and sober-minded men, who spoke only what they knew to be the truth.

If there be any weight in that train of argument which has been now sketched out, with a view of recommending it to general consideration, rather than fully developed, it follows, that those who confound together all religions with indiscriminate contempt, by speaking of them as all alike making pretensions to some divine revelation, are guilty of suppressing a most remarkable and essential distinction as to the character of those professed revelations: for if there be good ground for maintaining, first, that a false religion may be expected to contain in its pretended revelations superfluous matters, which concern only speculative curiosity; secondly, that all religions, except our own, do actually abound in such matters; thirdly, that a true revelation may be expected to *abstain* from every thing of the kind, and to contain only such things as are practically important, or, at least, nothing to gratify men's curiosity; and, lastly, that our Scriptures actually do conform to this rule; it will be difficult to avoid the conclusion, that they, and they only, do really come from God. Let this then not be omitted in the list of those many distinct proofs which combine to establish our faith; each one of which, besides its intrinsic force, augments (since they all tend to one common point) the strength of all the rest. No one, who judges correctly, and feels rightly, on the subject, will ever regard with indifference any valid argument, on the ground that he is already sufficiently convinced: for besides that he cannot tell what occasion he may hereafter find, on account of others, if not on his own; for any and every various kind of argument that can be adduced, (since different minds are influenced by different modes of proof,) it is, moreover, to a well-constituted mind, both profitable and delightful, to dwell on the contemplation of that vast mass of evidence which the Almighty has in this case provided; and *so* provided, that it shall not at once strike with its full force the most careless observer, but develop itself more and more, the further and the more diligently we pursue our enquiries in various directions.

In addition to the *evidence* for our religion which the view we have here taken may afford, there are some other not less important results to which it leads, as to the right use and right interpretation of Scripture; which it will be worth while briefly to hint at.

Let it be considered, then, first, what we ought to expect to learn from revelation; secondly, how we should understand what *is* revealed; and, lastly, what application we should make of it.

With respect to the first point, it is evident, from what has been said, that we must not expect to learn any thing from revelation, except what is in a *religious* point of view practically important for us to know.

Of other enquiries, there are some, (such as those respecting the laws of nature,) which it is safe and laudable to pursue by those other means which are within our reach; by the light of reason, aided by observation and experiment; only let no one seek for a system of astronomy, or of geology, or of any other branch of physical science, in the Scriptures, which were designed to teach men, not natural philosophy, but religion; nor let them be forced into the service of any particular theory on those subjects; nor, again, complained of, for not furnishing sufficient information on such points. Nor let any jealous fears be cherished, lest the pursuits of science should interfere with revelation. We may be confident, that a judicious and honest search after truth, conducted without any unfair prejudice, or insidious design, can never ultimately lead to any conclusion that is really irreconcileable with a true revelation: but so totally distinct are the objects respectively proposed, that innumerable varieties of opinion as to scientific subjects may, and in fact do, exist among men, who are all sincerely agreed in acknowledging the authority of Scripture.

There are other points again which are *not* within the reach of our natural faculties, but which, not being needful for us to know, and consequently not declared in revelation, are to be regarded as those " secret things which belong unto the Lord our God." As to such points, therefore, we should not only seek for no explanation in Scripture, but should carefully abstain from the presumption of all enquiry whatever. Many indeed of these " secret things" may perhaps no longer be such, in a future and higher state of existence; even though the same rule should still be observed, of not *miraculously revealing* any thing for the mere gratification of curiosity; for not only is it probable, that our faculties may be so far enlarged, as to enable us to understand and discover *for ourselves*, without direct revelation, things which at present surpass our powers; but also, it may be, that, in a different state of existence, many things may *become* of practical importance to us, which are not so now; and may thus become fit subjects of *revelation*. But in this present life we should carefully guard against the too prevailing error of presumptuous enquiries, and attempts to explain mysteries; an error which generally leaves men the more bewildered and mistaken, the greater their ingenuity and diligence.

Little as there is revealed to us of the condition of our first parents in Paradise, thus much (and let Christians never forget it) is plainly taught us, that they fell from their happy state through the desire of *forbidden knowledge*. It was by seeking from *men* to become "as *gods*, knowing good and evil," that they incurred that loss, to retrieve which God was made Man, in Christ Jesus; who "took upon him the form of a servant, and *humbled* himself unto death, even the death of the cross," to redeem us, the children of Adam, whom *want* of humility had ruined, and to open to us the gates of eternal life, which presumptuous transgression had shut. How then can we hope to enter in, if we repeat the very transgression of Adam, in seeking to know "the secret things which belong unto the Lord our God?" By inquisitive pride was immortal happiness forfeited; and the path by which we must travel back to its recovery is that of patient and resigned humility.

2. With respect to the right understanding of what *is* revealed, it is evident, if the view we have taken be correct, that the most *practical* interpretation of each doctrine that can fairly be adopted is ever likely to be the truest. Let it be laid down, therefore, as an important general rule, (of which numerous applications may be found by any one who will seek for them,) that if the other reasons be equal, or nearly equal, in favour of two different interpretations of any doctrine, one of which represents it as a mere speculative point of faith,

and the other as having some tendency to influence the heart or the conduct, this latter is to be adopted, as the more conformable to the general plan of revelation.

3. Lastly, if our religion be indeed of this practical character—if every thing revealed in it be intended to have an influence on our motives and actions—it behoves the Christian to be careful never to " put asunder what God has joined together;" but to make, and exhort others to make, a practical application of its doctrines to character and conduct. I mean, not merely that a virtuous life, as well as a right faith, is necessary; for though this is very true, it would have been no less true, if faith and practice had been *two totally distinct things, both* required of us;—if doctrines purely speculative had been proposed for our belief, and precepts un-connected with them subjoined : but as the case actually stands, it is not enough to say that the faith must be right, and the conduct right also; the conduct must *spring* from the faith; and not from some part of it only, but from all; the doctrines of our religion, not some of them, but all, must exert their influ-ence on the moral character.

That which was justly remarked by the Jewish historian, Josephus, of his own nation, may be applied with still more propriety to Christians, who are placed in the later and more complete form of the same general system; "while all other people," says he, "reckon religion a *part of virtue*, the Jews alone account virtue a *part of religion.*" I speak not now of the errors of those who *reject* either religious faith, or moral duty; but of those who regard them too much as *distinct*. There have indeed been many in all ages, from the ancient Peripatetic, down to the modern Deist, who have aimed at virtue without religion; and there have been many more, from the Pagan with his hecatombs and purifications, down to the Enthusiast of the present day, who have aimed at religion without virtue. But there are also some, it is to be feared, who though they acknowledge the necessity of both, are not sufficiently careful to keep in mind, and to exhibit, their close and intimate *connexion*; but (to use the illustration of St. James) separate from each other, as it were, the soul and the body, and yet think to preserve both. Else, we should not find so strong a distinction frequently drawn, between *doctrinal* and *practical discourses;* as if the two subjects were, neither of them indeed to be neglected, but kept apart and independent. Whereas in truth, every doctrinal discourse should lead the Christian hearer to its proper moral results— every practical precept be referred in his mind to its true foundation in the Gospel doctrines.

Such being then the practical character of Christianity, let it be observed in the last place, that all to whom the doctrines of Revelation have been taught, and those more especially whose attention has been more peculiarly directed to them by a course of theological studies, if they are not the better for their religious knowledge, will assuredly be the worse for it. It is not merely that, having failed to derive due advantage from the light of the Gospel, they will be heavily accountable for the neglect of so great a blessing; but by long familiarity with the doctrines of religion, while they neglect its duties, they will acquire a habit of insensibility to all moral impressions from that quarter: and by thus becoming hardened against the influence of the strongest of all motives, they will have shut the door against all hopes of reformation. For as those who have been long accustomed, for example, to encounter dangers, or to witness sufferings, without giving way to the corresponding emotions of fear or pity, are far more callous to such emotions, than those who have not been conversant with scenes of that kind ; so, those who have been long familiarized to the thoughts of religion, without applying it to their lives, are far more incurably hardened, than if they had never heard or thought any thing on the subject[f].

Let the Christian then never lose sight of that every way awful responsibility under which the Gospel revelation places him: ab-

---

[f] " Going over the theory of virtue, in one's thoughts—talking well—and drawing fine pictures of it—this is so far from necessarily or certainly conducing to form a habit of it in him who thus employs himself, that it may harden the mind in a contrary course, and form a habit of insensibility to all moral obligation. For from our very faculty of habits, passive impressions by being repeated, grow weaker, and thoughts, by often passing through the mind are felt less sensibly." *Bishop Butler's Sermons.*

staining from all unprofitable and presumptuous enquiries as to religious subjects, let him earnestly seek such knowledge as "is able to make us wise unto salvation, through faith which is in Christ Jesus;" and while in his *studies* he keeps in mind that "the secret things belong unto the Lord our God," let his *life* illustrate his conviction, that "the things which are revealed belong unto us, that we may *do* all the words of this Law."

The character of the revelation bestowed on us, in respect of the point which has just been considered, has a reference and a close correspondence, to another peculiarity of our religion—the proposal of the example of *children* by our sacred writers, with a view both to the explanation, and to the practical application, of what they teach. This peculiarity, by no means the least admirable in the Gospel-scheme, yet one which is in general very slightly noticed, will form the subject of the concluding Essay.

ESSAY V.

ON THE EXAMPLE OF CHILDREN AS PROPOSED TO CHRISTIANS.

THE allusion to the state of childhood, as illustrative of the condition and of the duties of Christians, occurs repeatedly in the sacred writings, and is dwelt on with an earnestness which may be regarded as one of the characteristic marks of the Gospel system of instruction.

Accordingly, many of our divines have occasionally alluded to the subject, and suggested it from time to time to the attention of their readers ; but the idea is not perhaps in general sufficiently expanded and dwelt upon in detail, to engage Christians to make it an habitual study, and resort continually for instruction to the example which is thus held out to them. And yet unless this be done—unless we dwell very fully and frequently on the case of children with a view to the better understanding of our own condition, and our own duties—we lose what is in fact one principal advantage of the example proposed to us, viz. its *commonness:* instead of selecting examples of rare and extraordinary virtue, or seeking to contemplate human nature under any peculiar and uncommon circumstances, we have only to look back to what we were ourselves when children, and to look around us to observe what children are. Neither learning nor genius are required for the study; and though the ablest man may derive from it such instruction as nothing else can supply, the plainest Christian may do the same, if he be but a sincere and candid and attentive enquirer.

The analogy now under consideration may be regarded as twofold: first, as children are in regard to their parents, so, in some respects, are we in relation to God: and, secondly, as children are in comparison of what they will be hereafter, so, in some respects, is the Christian in this present life, compared with what he hopes to be in the world to come. I say, in some respects, because it is not to be expected that whatever analogy may be presented to us should hold good throughout; and it is an important rule, never to press a comparison too far, nor to suppose that things which correspond in some points must therefore correspond in all. Thus, in the present instance, there is this important point of distinction between the two cases, that while children may expect to become hereafter what their parents are now, we, on the contrary, though in a certain sense the children of God, must always, even in the most exalted and glorified state to which we can attain in the next world, remain at an immeasurable distance from our Creator.

Yet notwithstanding this, our case is sufficiently analogous to that of children to furnish us with most valuable instruction, if we will but duly attend to the correspondence that does exist.

On many mysterious subjects, though man be unable to attain complete knowledge, he will thus at least be brought to understand the true nature and full extent of his own ignorance; and many of his duties will be most clearly pointed out and forcibly inculcated, by the example of children.

The subject is thus naturally divided into two branches; first, our analogy to children in respect of the *knowledge* we possess; and, secondly, in respect of *duties*—of the rules of conduct we may derive from contemplating the condition of childhood. On each of these points it is proposed not so much to offer instruction to the reader, as to lead him to instruct himself; not so much to enter into copious details, explaining what should be the Christian's judgment and what his conduct, in each case, as to suggest matter for his own private meditation and habitual observation. For the very object contemplated in holding out the example of children is, that men, by being referred to that example, may frame for themselves precepts more abundant and minute, and more exactly adapted to each particular case, than any that could be delivered to them by another.

I. In treating of the analogy of our situation to that of children in respect of knowledge, the circumstances to be noticed as most worthy of attention in the notions which they form, are these three; first, that their knowledge is, in *kind, relative; i.e.* that they know little more of any thing than the relation in which it stands to themselves : secondly, that in *degree,* it is a *scanty and imperfect* knowledge; and, thirdly, that it is nevertheless *practically* sufficient for them, if they are but careful to make a good use of it.

1. First then, with respect to the *kind* of knowledge which children possess : a few moments' consideration may convince us, that it is, as has been said, almost exclusively relative; *i. e.* that they know the nature of scarcely any thing, as it is *in itself*, but as it is *relatively* to *them*. A child soon becomes acquainted in some degree with its parents and other kindred—its nurses, teachers, and other friends ; but as to the nature of this knowledge, is it not manifest that it is merely relative? he knows little or nothing of what these persons really are, except so far as he himself is concerned with them ; he perceives in some measure what they are *to him;* but beyond this, he is nearly in the dark : the very words " parent," " kinsman," " friend," &c. are,

all of them, *relative* terms; and the notions belonging to these, and such as these, are the very earliest a child can form—these are the very first terms he is able in any degree to understand and apply.

Suppose the child's father to be some mighty sovereign, or an eminent statesman, poet, philosopher, or warrior—one whose life perhaps is of importance to millions, or whose fame spreads over half the globe; of all this the child himself has but a very faint, if any, conception; this Being, so great in station, or so remarkable in character, he regards merely as *his father;* this is but a *relation,* and is but one out of the many relations in which the same person stands to those around him; it is, however, the circumstance which is of the most consequence to the child himself; and it is, therefore, for a considerable time at least, the only one that he ever thinks about, or is at all capable of comprehending. As he grows older, fresh and fresh light is continually breaking in upon him, and he is continually gaining increased knowledge respecting the persons and the things that are around him; but still the main.

part of that knowledge, and all the earlier part of it, is relative, and relative to himself. Now we account it a mark of silly presumption in a child to pretend to understand fully, and pronounce upon positively, the nature of any thing as it is in itself; or to suppose that every thing is of greater or less importance in proportion as it affects himself. A child is indeed extremely apt to fall into this error; but we never fail to check it, and to endeavour to repress such a disposition, by explaining to him, as well as we can, how partial his knowledge is, even respecting those things of which he is not utterly ignorant, and how many there are which he cannot at present understand at all; we teach him, and strive to impress on his mind, that his friends have many other concerns to attend to besides what relates to him,—that he is not to measure the magnitude, nor judge of the nature, of every thing, merely with reference to himself,—and that even of those things which do principally concern him, and which are done for his sake, his knowledge and powers are so limited, that he must not reckon himself a competent judge of the fitness or unfitness of the measures that are taken. And we expect that a docile and well-disposed child will carefully listen to these admonitions, and will be so far sensible of his own weakness, as to perceive the propriety of complying with them.

Now Christians are surely called on to apply all this to themselves: especially when it is considered, that children approach incomparably nearer to an equality with their parents, than the creature can to the Creator; and that their knowledge of the character and transactions of grown persons is infinitely fuller and more perfect than we can have of the nature and dealings of God. Our knowledge of Him, like that of children, is almost entirely relative: the sacred writings, which hold out to us the condition of childhood as an illustration and as a pattern, these very Scriptures, with admirable consistency, reveal God to us, not as He is in Himself, but, chiefly, as He is in relation to ourselves. They tell us, that He is our Creator, Preserver, and Governor; that "in Him we live, and move, and have our being;" that "He is a rewarder of them that diligently seek

Him," and a judge that will punish those that disobey Him; that He took our nature upon Him in Christ Jesus to effect our salvation; and that He dwells in, and sanctifies, the hearts of his faithful servants. Now all this, and much more such knowledge, which the Scriptures supply to us respecting God, is evidently relative to ourselves. The very words, "Creator," "Governor," "Judge," "Redeemer," "Sanctifier," are altogether relative terms. And understanding imperfectly and indistinctly as we do this which is revealed, we may well expect to be utterly lost and bewildered when we attempt (going beyond revelation) to comprehend, by our own unaided powers, what God really is.

How, indeed, can our finite minds embrace infinity? The very words Omnipresence, and Eternity, overpower our faculties, the more, in proportion as they are dwelt upon; and yet we cannot conceive that God should *not* be present in every part of the universe which He created and maintains in its established order : wherever we go, we find traces of his agency ; yet we cannot either suppose Him to exist in any such relation to Space, that we and every thing around us has ; nor, again, conceive what that Being can be, who thus pervades all Space, and occupies none. We cannot, again, understand what it is to exist without any relation to Time ; yet we cannot but conclude, both from reason and revelation, that with Him, the Great I AM, there can be no distinction of Past, Present, and Future, but that all things must be eternally present ; since all our notions of time may be clearly traced up to the *succession* of ideas or impressions on our own minds ; which succession cannot be supposed to take place with an omniscient Being : so that the couplet of the poet Cowley, which has been, by some, laughed to scorn as absurd, will be found, if we duly consider it, to be the most appropriate expression possible of such imperfect and indistinct notions as alone we can entertain on such a subject :

> Nothing there is to come, and nothing past,
> But an eternal *now* does ever last.

Unfortunately, however, when men have affixed *names* to these indistinct and imperfect notions of theirs, and when, by long and frequent use, they have grown familiar with these names, they are thence apt to forget, how little they know of the *things* themselves. It is indeed a convenience to employ such names, provided we do not suffer ourselves to fancy, that the familiar use of them makes the things spoken of become intelligible. It is an advantage in algebraical calculations to employ a letter of the alphabet as a symbol to denote some unknown quantity; only let it not be supposed, that by this means it becomes at once a *known* quantity.

Moreover, besides the imperfect and indistinct knowledge which we have of those divine attributes whose existence we believe in, there may be others also, for ought we know, of which we have never had any suspicion, and which we should be as incapable of understanding with our present faculties, as a blind man is of forming any idea of colours. Is it not then something even worse than childish, to reason upon and discuss boldly, and pronounce upon dogmatically, the attributes and the acts of God? as if we had means of ascertaining the real nature of that stupendous

Being, instead of knowing merely, in some degree, what He is with respect to ourselves. It is true, that every one is ready to admit, in general terms, that the nature of God is not comprehensible by the human faculties; but how few are there that duly follow up this maxim in practice! how few writers, that, after having distinctly made the admission, do not, even within a few pages, slide imperceptibly into such a presumptuous style of assertion and of reasoning, as shews them to have completely forgotten that our knowledge of the Almighty is relative!

How great must be the errors arising from men's overlooking, or not carefully attending to, this circumstance, it is hardly necessary to point out: the rustic, who persists in maintaining that the sun itself actually moves, because he sees it rise and set, i. e. sees that it is in different *positions relatively to himself;* and the child, who, while he is sailing in a ship, fancies that the land flies from him, or advances towards him; are not more completely mistaken in their notions, than those theologians who reason upon the accounts which the Scriptures

give us of the Deity, as if these were intended
to explain to us what He is, absolutely, in
Himself, and not, merely what He is in relation
to ourselves. And the liability to error is
greatly increased by this circumstance; that
even the relations in which God stands to his
creatures are so imperfectly comprehensible
by our understandings, that it is necessary to
explain them by analogical language, and by
the use of such types and comparisons, as may
furnish to our minds a kind of picture or
image of heavenly things, whose correspondence with the original cannot of course be in
all points complete; any more than a picture
can*, in all respects, resemble the solid body
which it is designed to imitate. If therefore
we extend this analogy further than was intended, and conclude, that the things which
are represented as corresponding in some
points must needs correspond throughout,—or
if, again, we conclude, that the things must
be *alike*, because they are analogous, and bear

---

* See Archbishop King's Sermon on Predestination, already
referred to.

similar relations to something else,—we shall fall into the grossest absurdities; such as we often see in children, when they interpret literally the analogical explanations which are given them.

If any one will be at the pains to collect instances for himself (both from recollection of his own infancy, and from what he has observed in other children) of the mistakes which are in this way continually committed by every child, and will carefully reflect on these, not as a mere source of amusement, but with a view to his own instruction, they will serve as a mirror to shew what sort of mistakes he himself also has to guard against, in the notions he forms respecting the Almighty.

To take one out of innumerable instances; how many there are who speak and reason concerning the *glory* of God, (that being a phrase which occurs in Scripture,) as if they supposed, that the desire of glory did literally influence the divine mind, and as if God could really covet the admiration of his creatures: not considering, that the only intention of this expression is to signify merely, that God's works are contrived in the same admirable manner as if He *had* had this object in view; and that we are bound to pay Him the same reverent homage, and zealous obedience, as if He were really and literally capable of being glorified by us. And yet it is chiefly from a literal interpretation of this phrase of "the glory of God," that some Calvinistic divines have undertaken to explain the whole system of divine Providence, and to establish some very revolting and somewhat dangerous conclusions.

The considerations which have just been adduced lead naturally to a second point that is worthy of notice in the condition of children: not only is their knowledge almost entirely *relative*, but even of things relating to themselves they have a very *limited* knowledge; and what they do know, they know but imperfectly, partially, and indistinctly. It has been remarked above, that of their parents and kindred, and other friends, they know little or nothing except the relation in which these stand to themselves; but it is observable also, that this very relation they are far from adequately comprehending, so as to understand wherein it consists : and in this and every other part of their knowledge, those will usually appear to them the most *essential* circumstances, which, in fact, are *accidental*, or subordinate ; so that even where they are *not mistaken*, their knowledge is still very scanty and imperfect. For example, they will often learn accurately to distinguish from one another persons of different professions, by the colour of their clothes, or by some such external mark, which they are apt to regard as the real and essential characteristic of each, respectively; but as their faculties and knowledge improve, they come to perceive gradually, that what they had before considered as the most important circumstances, are subordinate, and comparatively trifling ; and that their former notions, though not altogether erroneous, were extremely defective, from their not being aware of, or perhaps even able to comprehend, those points which are in reality the most essential[b].

[b] It must strike every one who will please to review the ideas and imaginations of his youth, of what was then his notion of many things which he now looks at, and has long looked at,

Now let Christians but remember, that in this respect we are still children, in comparison of what Christ's faithful servants may hope to become in a future state; and that this process of not only rectifying errors, but clearing, and extending, and perfecting knowledge, is by no means yet completed, nor ever will be, in our present state. " When I was a child," says St. Paul, "I spake as a child, I thought as a child, I understood as a child; but when I

as so many vain and foolish baubles—how eager he was in the pursuit of them, how impatient of being disappointed. He is at a loss now to conceive where, or in what, the value or pleasure of them could consist, so much to engage his affections, to agitate his passions, to give him such anxiety in the pursuit, and pain in the loss. Now something very like this will probably take place in the judgment we shall hereafter form of many of the articles which at present compose the objects of our care and solicitude. When we come, in the new state of our existence, to look upon riches, and honours, and fortune, and pre-eminence, and prosperity—how like the play and pursuits of children, their little strifes, and contests, and disturbances, will these things appear? When the curtain is drawn aside, and the great scene of our future existence let in upon our view, how shall we regard the most serious of our present engagements and successes, as the toys and trifles of our childhood, the sport and pastime of this infancy of our existence! Paley's Sermons, last vol. p. 219, 220.

became a man, I put away childish things."
"We now," he adds, "see through a glass
darkly; but then face to face: now I know in
part; but then shall I know, even as also I am
known." When then, on the one hand, presumptuous objections are brought against the
received accounts, of the fall of man, for instance—of the redemption by Christ—of a future judgment—and every part of the divine
dispensations; and when, on the other hand,
no less presumptuous explanations are offered
of the same; let him, who would derive wisdom
from the source which God has pointed out,
instead of listening either to such objections,
or to such answers, occupy himself in reflect-
ing on the absurd mistakes which children
commit, when they imagine themselves to have
a full and correct notion of any thing that has
been partially explained to them, and suffer
themselves to fancy (as soon as any glimmering of knowledge has been afforded them) that
they understand completely the transactions
and situations of grown persons. And if any
one would attain the best idea he is capable of
forming on that most important point of wis-

dom, the nature and extent of his own ignorance, let him seek it by analogy, and have recourse to a child for his instructor: let him endeavour to convey to a very young child as full and correct a notion as possible of civil government, and legal institutions—of commercial transactions, and various arts and sciences—of the past history and present condition of various nations; and let him carefully observe how utterly unintelligible many points will remain to the infant mind, after all the explanations that can be given; how *uninteresting* many subjects will prove, which hereafter will be regarded as the most important; how imperfect and inadequate will be the notions that are formed on others, and what strange mistakes will be continually arising; especially if the child, through conceit and presumption, is not aware of his own incompetency to judge, and does not perceive that he is out of his depth. And then let the instructor apply the lesson to himself: let him learn from the example of the child what is likely to be the imperfection of his own knowledge and of his own faculties; and let him no longer presume that he understands, or can expect to discover, the whole, or even the greater and more essential part, of any one of the divine dispensations[c], merely on the ground

[c] " We can seldom review what passed in our minds when we were children, without being surprised with the odd and extravagant notions which we took up and entertained—how wildly we accounted for some things, and what strange forms we assigned to many other things—what improbable resemblances we supposed, what unlikely effects we expected, what consequences we feared. I can easily believe, that many of the opinions and notions we now erroneously entertain, especially concerning the place, condition, nature, occupation, and happiness of departed saints, may hereafter appear to us as wild, as odd, as unlikely and ill-founded, as our childish fancies appear to us now. Like the child, we take our ideas from what we see, and transfer them to what we do not see; like him, we look upon and judge of things above our understanding, by comparing them with things which we do understand; and they bear afterwards as little resemblance, as little foundation for comparison, as the most chimerical and fantastic visions of a childish imagination. And this I judge to be what St. Paul had particularly in his thoughts when he wrote the words of the text: ' Now we know in part; but when that which is perfect is come, then that which is in part shall be done away;' even as ' when I was a child, I understood as a child, I thought as a child; but when I became a man, I put away childish things.' Our apprehension of futurity may, it is true, be in many respects childish, but still

that some part of God's designs has been declared to him; nor flatter himself, that because he is assured of the truth of *something*, therefore there is nothing that is concealed from him.

A child perceives that the sun gives light and heat to the spot which he inhabits; so far he judges rightly; but he is not unlikely to conclude, that the sun was created for that purpose; he is ignorant of its conferring the same advantages on distant parts of the world; and he supposes its real magnitude to be nearly the same as it appears to be: by degrees his knowledge is enlarged, and he comes to understand, that the same sun shines upon the whole earth; he now perhaps looks back with contempt on his former ignorance, and imagines that he understands fully the whole use and importance of the sun; whereas he still knows but a very small part of it: in time, if he is in

they may be innocent, so long as we are not over anxious, nor over positive, to insist upon others receiving them, and too much inclined to make difficulties, or start at those which we meet with, from an opinion that we are able to guess and find out the whole of such subjects." Paley's Sermons, last vol. p. 223, 224.

the way of scientific instruction, and is diligent in profiting by it, he will come to learn, that the earth is only one out of many planets—several much larger than our own—that are warmed and enlightened by the same sun, which is a far larger body than all of them together; and we should be very presumptuous were we to conclude, that even this purpose is the sole, or even the principal one, for which the sun was created. Most arrogant then must he be, who dares conclude, that when he knows something of God's attributes and dispensations, he fully understands either the whole, or even the most essential part, of them. We know certain relations in which the Almighty stands towards us; but there may be other relations besides these, of which we know nothing: we are instructed in some degree how far we are interested in the fall of Adam, in the redemption through Christ, and in other of God's dispensations; but we know not that this is all; nor have we any reason for supposing, that even the greater part has been revealed to us. The fall of our first parents may, for ought we know, have been of consequence to different orders of Beings, whose very existence we are ignorant of; the death of Christ may, in some unknown way, be the means of salvation to millions who never heard of Him; his coming to judge the world may affect other planets besides our own. Is this vast extent of ignorance revolting to any one? let him then recollect the time when he was a child, and refresh his memory by the observation of other children; let him remember, how strange many things seemed to him, which are now perfectly cleared up; how utterly ignorant he was of matters, which are now familiar to him; how far he was from being able to comprehend the nature, and even from suspecting the existence, of many things, which now principally occupy his thoughts; and, above all, how sure he was to be mistaken, whenever he presumed to fancy that his own notions were adequate, and his knowledge perfect. This habitual study of the infantine mind will prepare us to go any lengths in the confession of our ignorance, and the due distrust of our faculties: we shall thus become learned in human nature, as to that most important part of it, its imperfections;

and where full and accurate knowledge is not to be attained, we shall at least keep clear of presumptuous error. Where the darkness cannot be removed, it is a great point to be aware that it *is* darkness, instead of being deceived and misled by false lights and delusive appearances.

It was mentioned as a third point in which the knowledge possessed by children is worthy of consideration, that, scanty and imperfect as it is, it is yet fully sufficient for all practical purposes; a child knows indeed but little of the friends that surround him; but he knows enough to understand that they *are* friends, and that he may profit by their instructions, and rely on their protection. Children soon learn to distinguish in a great degree what things are agreeable, and what, painful; what profitable, and what, mischievous; and if they are patient and docile, they rapidly improve in this kind of knowledge. They learn also very early, what sort of conduct will gain them the approbation and goodwill of their parents and their play-fellows, and what will subject them to displeasure, ridicule, or punishment. Almost all the knowledge indeed that is early and easily acquired by children, is of a practical nature. For example, a child, as has been above remarked, understands very little of the real nature of the sun; but he very soon comes to understand its efficacy in enlightening—in warming—in drying—in altering the colours of several substances—in expanding flowers—in ripening fruits. This sort of knowledge it is, universally, that is the most essential to be early acquired; and it is of such knowledge consequently, that, by the appointment of Providence, children are the most capable. That which they can best learn, as children, is precisely such as is best calculated to lead them on to a more advanced state, and to qualify them for their future conduct in the world as men.

Such likewise is our state in this present life; we can attain abundant knowledge for practical purposes; in the midst of all our ignorance and weakness, that which we can *best* understand is our *duty:* and if we are diligent and patient in acquiring such knowledge as is suitable for us, and in practically applying it, instead of boldly prying into mysteries beyond our reach, we shall be undergoing the best preparation for that superior state of existence, in which God's faithful servants will, through his mercy, obtain an enlargement of their faculties, an increase of their knowledge, and a nearer view of his adorable perfections. On the other hand, the evils which are brought upon the *man* by presumptuous disobedience, by carelessness, and by indocility, in the child may warn us what those have to expect, who, in what concerns religion, copy the example of such perverseness.

II. This reference of knowledge to practice, leads naturally to the consideration of that which was laid down as the second branch of the present enquiry, viz. the advantages to be derived from a comparison between the condition of Christians and that of children, in respect of *conduct;* their example being often held out for *imitation* by Jesus and his followers; whose manner of teaching is in this respect hardly less peculiar than in the others formerly mentioned. In treating of the former branch of the subject before us, the object proposed may be described as being to shew how far men *necessarily are* like children : how far *they ought to be so*—what instruction they may derive in respect of duty, from following the example of children—is our present matter of consideration.

The disciples, we are told in the Gospel, came unto Jesus, saying, "Who is the greatest in the kingdom of heaven? and Jesus called a little child unto Him, and set him in the midst of them, and said, Verily I say unto you, except ye be converted, and become as little children, ye shall not enter into the kingdom of heaven. Whosoever therefore shall humble himself as this little child, the same is the greatest in the kingdom of heaven." Our Lord's most immediate object seems to have been, to check the pride of his disciples ; we may presume therefore that the point in which He was more especially holding out children to our imitation, is their lowliness of mind, modesty, and self-distrust.

To this must be added, in the second place, their *docility* ; *i. e.* a disposition to listen with

candour, and singleness of heart, and patience,
to the instruction that is imparted to them. It is
thus that St. James reasons from the *filial* relation in which we stand to God : "of his own
will," says he, (chap. i. 18—21.) "*begat He us*
with the word of truth, that we should be a kind
of first fruits of his creatures. Wherefore, my
beloved brethren, let every man be *swift to
hear, slow to speak,* slow to wrath; (for the
wrath of man worketh not the righteousness of
God.) Wherefore lay apart all filthiness and
superfluity of naughtiness, and receive with
meekness the engrafted word, which is able to
save your souls."

Lastly, another point, in which the example of children is most profitable for the
imitation of Christians, is that which may be
called their *resignation;* i. e. an undoubting
and affectionate confidence in parental care
and kindness; accompanied with a cheerful
submission and ready obedience, even where
they cannot understand the reasons of the commands given, and of the restrictions imposed.

1. First then, with respect to the humility of
children : though we do indeed frequently find

in them the seeds of arrogance, as well as of every other evil propensity to which our frail and corrupt nature is liable; it will hardly be denied, that, as a general rule, childhood is characterised by modesty, self-distrust, consciousness of weakness, and readiness to acknowledge faults: they are qualities also peculiarly *suitable* to that age; and we are accordingly especially careful to warn children against presumption and self-confidence, and to impress them with a due sense of their own ignorance, and inexperience, and feebleness. Now if it be true, as has been above pointed out, that the Christian's condition in this present life is closely analogous to that of children—that we are still in the infancy of our being, compared with what we hope to become hereafter—and that we are, and ever must be, children, and much less than children, in respect of our Creator—it is evidently the part of one, who would profit by this most important branch of knowledge, to exemplify in himself that conduct which he most commends in them, and to apply to himself the precepts he inculcates. If humility is especially becoming in a child, it must be so also in a Christian, who is made in a peculiar manner "a child of God;" thus placed in the relation of sonship towards a Being infinitely more above him than an earthly parent: if a child is exposed to the greatest mischiefs both in his present state, and in his future life, by arrogant presumption, and conceited confidence in his own feeble judgment, let man, weak and short-sighted as he is, remember, that the same faults in him will endanger his eternal salvation.

Having already dwelt at greater length, perhaps, than some may think requisite, on the imperfection of the human faculties, and the scantiness of man's knowledge in his present state, it is unnecessary to insist strongly in this place on the importance of that humble self-distrust, consciousness of ignorance, and lowliness of temper, which are called for in consequence. But there is one point most important to be kept in view, which many men are apt to overlook; those, viz. who imagine themselves to be not at all deficient in humility, provided they abstain from over-rating their own talents as *compared with those of other* men: whereas it is evidently possible for a man to possess this *personal* humility, as it may be called—to think very modestly of himself in comparison of those around him, and yet greatly to over-rate the *human faculties* in *general*; and without giving himself credit for acuteness and profundity beyond the rest of the species, to be guilty of rashly prying into the mysteries of the Most High, and of speculating boldly on subjects which are out of the reach, perhaps, even of the faculties of angels. No cautions against *personal* arrogance will guard a man against this (if I may so speak) *generic* arrogance—this over-estimate of the human faculties. No man must be satisfied with thinking modestly of himself, individually, as compared with others, unless he also form as sufficiently humble estimate of human nature itself; recollecting that the whole race of mankind are in a state of ignorance and weakness analogous to that of childhood.

2. The second point which was mentioned, as deserving the imitation of Christians, is the docility of children; the docility which we always find, at least in those of them who are

the best disposed; and which we always commend them for possessing, and studiously inculcate. It is not enough for a child to acknowledge his imperfections, if he has no wish to improve; nor to be conscious of his ignorance, unless he is willing to learn. In fact, as there is no greater obstacle to improvement—no worse impediment to learning—than arrogant self-conceit, so there is no better proof of modesty, than an eagerness to receive instruction. If we inculcate humility, it is as a step—the first and most important step—towards the attainment of excellence: those children who conceitedly over-rate themselves, and shew no deference for the precepts bestowed on them, are often the least ambitious, and always the least likely, to make great advancements.

Now if the Christian acknowledge himself to be at all in the condition of children, he should learn in this point also most carefully to take pattern from them, and to practise what he recommends to them; for while they have to learn what will qualify them for the state of manhood—for that short and precarious life which they will have to spend on earth—the Christian has to learn, according to the views which the Gospel presents, what may fit him for eternity: on the use he makes of the short time of probation allowed him here, in acquiring a knowledge of the will of God, and in applying that knowledge in his practice—on this it is, that his condition, his final and unalterable condition, in the next world, is represented in the Scriptures as depending.

He then who is taught such a lesson by a master to whose authority he bows, must admit that the example of children, and the advice men are perpetually inculcating on them, will rise up against him in the day of judgment and condemn him, if his conduct in this his state of infancy be such as he would, in his own children, censure as most culpable folly. How strongly, for example, and how justly, does every one blame a child who refuses to learn or believe any thing that does not suit his own inclinations; who will not take any thing *upon trust*, even when he is incompetent at present to understand the reasons of it, nor believe implicitly what he cannot fully comprehend, even though assured of it on the safest authority; and who arrogantly denies and rejects every thing that carries with it an appearance of difficulty, unless that difficulty be instantly and satisfactorily solved.

This example is well calculated to warn the Christian to beware, lest he lie open to the same blame in a far more important concern; remembering, that as Jesus Christ himself teaches him, " if he receive not the kingdom of heaven as a little child, he shall in no wise enter therein."

There are, indeed, many Christians, who, (not, certainly, for want of having an instructive model recommended to their imitation in Scripture, but for want of studying that model,) instead of this childlike simplicity, and singleness of heart, and candour, are perpetually striving to fashion the word of God according to their own imaginations: perverting and explaining away every passage which does not suit their preconceived notions, and pressing, to the utmost extreme, every one that seems to support them; rejecting *this* doctrine, because it appears to them unreasonable—and *that,* because it is, on their views, unworthy of the Deity—and *another*, because it is attended with some inexplicable difficulty; or insisting with uncharitable vehemence on the importance of some particular explanation, founded on the deductions of their own reason, and forming an essential part of their own theory; making no allowance even for one who substantially agrees with them, if it happen that he does not employ precisely the same form of expression; or if he contentedly believes, without being able to comprehend, what they profess to have explained.

" What then," it may be said, " is all employment of reason to be abandoned, and are we to teach, with the Romanists, the virtue of implicit and unenquiring faith? Are we to learn from children boundless credulity, and contented ignorance?" A child himself can answer the objection, and remove whatever difficulty it involves. Ask an intelligent child whether his parents exhort him to remain contented in ignorance—to believe implicitly every thing that every one tells him, whether on good authority or not; to abstain from all enquiry—to repress all curiosity—and to use no endeavours for improving in knowledge, and attaining truth. He will tell you, that, so far from this, they commend him for nothing more than for being properly inquisitive, and eager after information; that they exhort him to take nothing upon trust that he is capable of sifting thoroughly, and examining and proving satisfactorily to himself; and that they assiduously warn him against being over-credulous, and hasty in admitting on slender proofs what he hears from persons undeserving of credit. He will tell you, however, that they nevertheless caution him against an indiscriminate, and presumptuous, and prying curiosity; that they assure him there are some points of knowledge unsuitable to his age; and many which are beyond the reach of his present faculties, which it would be unprofitable, and even mischievous, for him to pry into unseasonably; that he must wait with patience till his reason is matured; since there is enough of what is necessary and useful for him to learn, to occupy all his attention in the mean time; and that even of what he has to learn at present, there are many parts which he cannot as yet fully comprehend; and which therefore he must be content to believe implicitly, on the authority of his instructors, in whose veracity and judgment he has the best reason to confide.

Is not this the system of instruction which is adopted by the most judicious teachers? and is there any thing inconsistent in this? Is it not possible at once to encourage profitable, and to repress impertinent, curiosity? To check indiscriminate credulity, yet to require implicit faith, (on sufficient authority,) on subjects beyond the reach of the learner's faculties—and to encourage enquiry about such as are *not* beyond his reach? Now if this be the wisest and best way of instructing children, can we doubt, or can we wonder, or can we complain, that our great Master, " our Father which is in heaven," has adopted this same method in the instruction of us, in our present state of childhood here on earth?

The Christian is taught in the Scriptures he receives, and most wisely taught, to make it his careful and constant study to distinguish what subjects are, and what are not, within the reach of his faculties; that while he avoids presumptuous enquiries, he may at the same time be diligently pursuing such knowledge as is attainable and profitable.

There have been indeed sceptical philosophers, who have perversely inferred, from the limited and imperfect nature of the human faculties, that all enquiries after truth are vain; and have thought, or pretended to think, that since we understand so little of any subjects on which we may speculate, we ought to sit down contented in universal doubt, and universal indifference, respecting all. But it is surely something even beyond a childish absurdity to conclude, that because we cannot do all we wish, we therefore should do nothing at all; that because we are aware of the limits of our faculties, therefore we should not employ them as far as they extend. A man who is compelled to travel in the twilight, may *wish* indeed that the sun would rise; but in the mean time makes the best use he can of the light that *is* afforded him; he still employs his eyes, and still is able to see with them, to a profitable purpose; though he cannot see so far as in broad day-light: only, if he is prudent, he will take heed not to forget how faint a glimmering it is that he now enjoys, lest he incur danger by heedlessly running too far from the path; nor will he allow himself to form too hasty a judgment concerning the prospect around him, while viewed by this imperfect light.

The Christian then, though warned not to attempt to be " wise *above* what is written," is yet excited by the very same example, diligently to study and strive to improve in the knowledge of that which God *has* thought fit to reveal in this life; hoping to attain a more perfect knowledge in a better state. And if he would resemble, in all that is worthy of imitation, such a child as he would wish his own children to be, he will come to the study with a disposition meekly and candidly to receive the word of God, whatever he shall find it to be: not searching the Scriptures for arguments to confirm his preconceived opinions; but honestly forming his opinions *from* what he reads; and cheerfully acquiescing in whatever he may find to be revealed, however repugnant to the prejudices and galling to the pride, of human nature. *That* faith, without which the Scriptures tell us "it is impossible to please God"—which they uniformly represent as of the nature of a moral virtue, and as the first step in the Christian's progress—does not consist (as the scoffing infidel pretends) in assenting to a proposition *without* sufficient evidence, but in a disposition candidly and fairly to *weigh* the evidence—in a due distrust of the human faculties—and in a readiness to admit whatever shall appear to be clearly taught by our divine Instructor, even though it be such as we should never have expected, nor can clearly comprehend. Such is the *docility* which men require of children, and which they approve and commend in them ; and such also is the docility which they must require of themselves, if they would obtain the approbation of their heavenly Father.

3. The last and not least important point in which the example of children is to be imitated, is that which has been called their *resignation :* I mean, the entire, devoted, contented, and affectionate submission of a well disposed child to his parent's will ; his ready and cheer-

ful obedience, even to commands of which he cannot understand the reason; his full and contented confidence in parental care and kindness, even in cases where his father's conduct is unintelligible to him.

Every one knows how many things it is necessary for children to do, and to submit to, of which they cannot, at the time, understand the necessity: and we should not much commend the dutiful obedience of that child, who should then only submit to his parent's will, when he comprehended the reasons of his commands: nor should we think well of a child's disposition, whose affections were alienated from a tender parent, and who distrusted that parent's kindness, merely on the ground of his being obliged to practise some irksome duties, and submit to some troublesome restraints, whose importance could not as yet be explained to him. Let any one but consider, which of the two would be regarded as the more amiable and the more sensible child—such an one as this last, or the one before described, as full of confidence, love, and submission. And if the Christian feels no hesitation in deciding this question, let him next consider, which of the two it behoves him to resemble.

Placed as man is at an immeasurable distance from the stupendous Author of our being, and in a state of infancy, compared with the future life he looks forward to, it may well be expected that he should be incapable of understanding the reasons of all God's commands, and the whole system of his dealings with his creatures. But enough may surely be understood, to convince those who are well disposed, that they may safely trust to his fatherly care and goodness—that He deserves our sincere affection and devoted obedience—and that "all things work together for good to them that love Him." It is therefore man's duty, as well as interest, cheerfully to comply with his will, even when he neither knows the reason of his commands, nor understands why that knowledge is withheld from him. Though thus much all may clearly understand; that if this life be a state of *probation*, as every thing around us declares that it is, we might even antecedently expect, that, among other moral qualities, a trial should be made of our humility also, of our patience, of our devotion to God, and firm trust in Him; a trial which could not take place, if men could in every instance fully understand the wisdom of the Almighty Ruler's designs, and perceive the fitness of his injunctions. The Christian then is evidently called upon in this point also, to pursue the same conduct himself which he recommends in children; *resigning* himself with affectionate devotion into the hands of God; not presuming to find fault with any thing he does not understand, nor giving way to distrust, wherever he perceives a difficulty [d].

[d] " A child meets with perpetual difficulties, which appear to its then comprehension unconquerable, which yet, when it becomes a man, clear up and vanish of themselves. It cannot be made to understand the reason or the meaning of half the things which its parents and its masters make it do or suffer. . . . .

" How is this to be reconciled, a child will naturally ask, with that kindness, and love, and goodness, which it is told to expect from its parents. Now as the child advances in reason and observation, all these difficulties solve themselves. He remembers with gratitude what he suffered with complaint. . . . .

" Look to the whole of our existence, and the wisest and

Some, however, find means practically to evade the force of that lesson, which the example of children is intended to convey. That a child is right in shewing filial affection, and in submitting to parental authority, they see and acknowledge, on the ground that they themselves perceive that this is for his benefit; whereas *they* do *not* perceive how God's de-

oldest of us are yet but in our infancy...... We know in part; a certain portion of our nature, existence, and destiny we do see; but it is a portion bounded by narrow limits;—a term out of eternity. Now all such partial knowledge must be encumbered with many difficulties; it is like viewing the map of a district, or small tract of territory, by itself, and separated from the adjacent country: we see rivers marked out, without any source to flow from, and running where there is nothing to receive them. In like manner we observe events in the world, of which we trace not either cause or origin, and tending to no design or purpose that we can dis- cover. If the child have patience to wait, many of these diffi- culties will in due time be explained. And this is our case. It was not necessary to the child's happiness and well-being, that it should have, from the first, the understanding of a man; nor is it to ours, that we should possess the faculties of angels, or those which are in reversion for us in a higher and more advanced state of existence." Paley's Sermons.

He is indebted, however, to Tucker's " Light of Nature," for the admirable illustration just cited.

signs tend to their benefit : not considering,
that neither can the child himself fully understand this, at the time ; but implicitly takes it
for granted. Now if we are in a condition
analogous to childhood, we must put ourselves
in the place of the *child himself*, not of a *bye-
stander*, whose knowledge of the circumstances
is more complete : we must consider, not
merely whether the conduct of the child does
in fact tend eventually to his own benefit, and
is such as a person *would* direct, who knew
better than the child himself can know, wherein
the benefit consists ; but we must also consider,
whether the child himself, even with the imperfect knowledge which *he* now possesses, does
not act wisely in submitting and trusting to
his parent ; and if it be decided that he *has*
good reason for so doing, it is incumbent on
those who are in a corresponding condition,
and have the same imperfect knowledge, to
follow his example. For if man in his present
state *could* fully perceive and understand that
what is commanded him is for his good, his
case would *not* then be analogous to that of
children ; since *they cannot*, while children,

understand the designs of their parents. The question is therefore, is it a mark of folly in children, to be dutiful, affectionate, and submissive? Shall we say that such children are *right* indeed, but right only by *accident*, in thus trusting to their parents; and that they have, at the time when they do so, no just ground for reposing such confidence in them? No one would surely maintain such an opinion. If then we acknowledge the conduct of dutiful children to be wise—wise, that is, under the circumstances in which they are placed—it is for us to make it the pattern of our own. An amiable, and well disposed, and intelligent child never reasons in this manner; "My father's designs are inscrutable to me, and therefore I cannot tell whether the steps he may next take will be for my benefit, or the contrary: he *may* have very good reasons for all he does; but since I cannot understand his reasons for occasionally subjecting me to pain and privation, I cannot tell but that he may hereafter see sufficient reasons, equally unintelligible to me, for devoting me undeservedly to misery and destruction; and therefore I have no ground for trusting to his kindness:" such, I say, are not the reasonings which pass through the mind of a well-disposed child; who, notwithstanding his incapacity to explain to himself the reasons of his being sometimes exposed to pain and inconvenience, feels, nevertheless, an undoubting confidence (and surely it is not an unreasonable and ill-grounded confidence) that his father loves him, and seeks his real benefit, and understands how to promote it far better than he does himself.

The disciple of Christ then is taught to profit by such an example; and, without being dismayed by his inability to explain the evils which appear in the creation*, to trust fully (as

---

* The sentiments here expressed, are more fully developed and explained in the Appendix (No. 2.) to Dr. King's Discourse on Predestination; from which I take the liberty of citing one passage, as necessary to illustrate what has been said: " Our notions of the moral attributes of the Deity are not derived (as Dr. Paley contends they are) from a bare contemplation of the created universe, without any notions of what is antecedently probable, to direct and aid our observations. Nor is it true (few indeed would now, I apprehend, assent to that part of his doctrine) that man has no moral faculty—no natural principle of preference for virtue rather

he has good reason) in the loving-kindness of God towards those who diligently serve Him;

than vice—benevolence rather than malice; but that being compelled by the view of the universe to admit that God is benevolent, is thence led, from prudential motives alone, to cultivate benevolence in himself, with a view to secure a future reward. The truth I conceive is exactly the reverse of this; viz. that man having in himself a moral faculty, or taste, as some prefer to call it, by which he is instinctively led to approve virtue and disapprove vice, is thence disposed and inclined antecedently, to attribute to the Creator of the universe, the most perfect and infinitely highest of beings, all those moral (as well as intellectual) qualities which to himself seem the most worthy of admiration, and intrinsically beautiful and excellent: for to do evil rather than good, appears to all men (except to those who have been very long hardened and depraved by the extreme of wickedness) to imply something of weakness, imperfection, corruption, and degradation. I say, "*disposed* and *inclined*," because our admiration for benevolence, wisdom, &c. would not *alone* be sufficient to make us attribute these to the Deity, if we saw *no* marks of them in the creation; but our finding in the creation many marks of contrivance, and of beneficent contrivance, *together with* the antecedent bias in our own minds, which inclines us to attribute goodness to the supreme Being—*both these conjointly*, lead us to the conclusion that God is infinitely benevolent, notwithstanding the admixture of evil in his works, which we cannot account for. But these appearances of evil would stand in the way of such a conclusion, if man really were, what Dr. Paley represents him, a being destitute of all moral who conform cheerfully to his commandments, and who rely firmly on his promises.

sentiment, all innate and original admiration for goodness: he would in that case be more likely to come to the conclusion (as many of the heathen seem actually to have done) that the Deity was a being of a mixed or of a capricious nature; an idea which, shocking as it is to every well-constituted mind, would not be so in the least, to such a mind as Dr. Paley attributes to the whole human species. To illustrate this argument a little further, let us suppose a tasteful architect and a rude savage to be both contemplating a magnificent building, unfinished, or partially fallen to ruin; the one, not being at all able to comprehend the complete design, nor having any taste for its beauties if perfectly exhibited, would not attribute any such design to the author of it, but would suppose the prostrate columns and rough stones to be as much designed as those that were erect and perfect; the other would sketch out in his own mind something like the perfect structure of which he beheld only a part; and though he might not be able to explain how it came to be unfinished or decayed, would conclude that some such design was in the mind of the builder: though this same man, if he were contemplating a mere rude heap of stones which bore *no* marks of design at all, would not in *that* case draw such a conclusion. Or again, suppose two persons, one having an ear for music, and the other totally destitute of it, were both listening to a piece of music imperfectly heard at a distance, or half drowned by other noises, so that only some notes of it were distinctly caught, and others were totally lost or heard imperfectly; the one might suppose that the sounds he heard were all that were

And let it not be forgotten, that that feature in the Gospel-system of instruction which has been here noticed, the proposal of such an example for man's imitation in his present state, is one of the circumstances *peculiar* to *Christianity*—strikingly characteristic of it—and strongly confirming its divine origin, its importance, and its excellence.

As it is obviously a great advantage to teach not merely by precept, but by example, so, that advantage is much enhanced, if the ex-

actually produced, and think the whole that met his ear to be exactly such as was designed; but the other would form some notion of a piece of real music, and would conclude that the interruptions and imperfections of it were not parts of the design, but were to be attributed to his imperfect hearing: though if he heard, on another occasion, a mere confusion of sounds without any melody at all, he would not conclude that any thing like music was designed.

"The application is obvious: the wisdom and goodness discernible in the structure of the universe, but imperfectly discerned, and blended with evil, leads a man who has an innate approbation of those attributes, to assign them to the Author of the universe, though he be unable to explain that admixture of evil; but if man were destitute of moral sentiments, the view of the universe, such as it appears to us, would hardly lead him to that conclusion."

ample employed be one which is *always at hand:* nor could a more *suitable* pattern, than the one in question, have been presented to the imitation of creatures, standing in such a relation as we do to the Creator; and whose present life is designed as a preparation for a more perfect and exalted state hereafter. Yet the best heathen moralists, even those who taught and professed to believe a future state, had not recourse to, or at least did not usually employ, this mode of instruction. They spoke much of the beauty of virtue—of the dignity of human nature—of the heroism of striving to rise above the vulgar mass of mortals: but they did not enough consider, that the first step to elevation is *Humility;* that though the palace of Wisdom be indeed a lofty structure, its entrance is low, and it forbids admission without bending: they knew not, or at least taught not, that our nature must be exalted by first understanding and acknowledging the full amount of its weakness and imperfection. " Jesus called unto Him a little child, and set him in the midst:" what other teacher ever did the like? What other teacher indeed ever completely " knew what was in man," and understood throughly how to remedy the defects of his nature, and to fit him for a better state?

While this admirable peculiarity of our great Master's system of instruction is gratefully acknowledged by the Christian, let him be careful also to take advantage of it, and not to lose the benefit of the example which Christ has proposed for our imitation. It is not enough to acknowledge in general terms that man's condition on earth is analogous to that of children, in the scantiness of his knowledge, and the imperfection of his faculties ; and that we ought to take pattern from their humble docility, and cheerful confidence, and implicit obedience: he who would actually profit by this pattern, must make their character and conduct his habitual study—a study which no one can ever want opportunities of pursuing. We must " call a little child, and set him in the midst of us :" we must carefully and frequently examine into all the details of the condition, the character, and duties, of children : and if we are fully and habitually impressed with the similarity of our situation to theirs, in a multitude of particulars, then, and then only, we shall be enabled to profit adequately by the example they afford us.

By such a moral training will the Christian be fitted, through God's help, for that more perfect, that happy and exalted, state, in which his doubts will be dispelled, his knowledge cleared up and extended, his faith swallowed up in certainty, and his nature purified and elevated so as to approach more nearly to that of his divine Master. " Brethren," says St. John, " we know not what we shall be ; but we know, that, when He shall appear, we shall be *like* Him ; for we shall see Him as He is."

APPENDIX.

APPENDIX.

ONE of the most remarkable and least noticed of the peculiarities of the Christian Religion has been omitted in the preceding Essays, as having been treated of in a Discourse delivered at Oxford on the 5th of November, 1821, which, with four others, I subjoined to the second edition of the Bampton Lectures. A brief notice, however, of the subject and outline of the argument, connected as it is with the object of this volume, may not be unsuitably subjoined to it.

The peculiarity alluded to is, that *the Christian Religion alone is without a Priest*. The ambiguity of language, and also the erroneous practice of some Christian Churches, render it necessary to offer proofs of an assertion, which when distinctly understood, and applied to the religion as taught in Scripture, is at once evident.

It is well known, that certain ministers of religion were ordained by Christ and his apostles, and have continued in an unbroken succession down to the present day: and it is not to be wondered at, that the *name* " Priest " should be applied in common to these and to the *ministers* of every other religion, true or false: but the point to be observed is, that their *office* is essentially and fundamentally different. When the title is applied, for instance, to a Jewish priest, and to a Christian, it is applied equivocally; not to denote two different *kinds* of priests, but in two different senses; the essential circumstances which *constitute* the priestly office in the one, being wanting in the other. Accordingly, there are in Greek, as is well known, two words, totally unconnected in etymology, which are used to denote the two offices respectively; the Jewish priest, and also that of the Pagan religions, being invariably called ΙΕΡΕΥΣ; the Christian priest, ΠΡΕΣΒΥΤΕΡΟΣ, (or sometimes ΕΠΙΣΚΟΠΟΣ,) from which our English word " Priest" is manifestly formed. It is remarkable, however, that it is never rendered " Priest" in our version of the Bible, but always according to its etymology, " Elder;" and that wherever the word Priest occurs, it is always used to correspond to 'Ιερεύς. This last title is applied frequently to Jesus Christ himself, but never to any other character under the Gospel-dispensation. This circumstance alone would render it highly probable, that Christ and his apostles did not intend to institute in the Christian Church any office corresponding to that of priest in the Jewish: otherwise they would doubtless have designated it by a name so familiarly known. And if we look to the doctrines of their religion, we shall plainly see that they could have had no such intention. For it was manifestly the essence of the priest's office (both in the true religion of Moses, and in the Pagan imitations of the truth) to offer Sacrifice and Atonement for the people—to address the Deity on their behalf as a

Mediator and Intercessor—and to make a Propitiation for
them. All these are described as belonging to Christ,
and to Him alone, under the Gospel-dispensation; which
consequently (alone of all religions we are acquainted
with) has, on earth, no Priest at all.

The office of the Christian ministers, the Elders or
Presbyters, which the apostles by their divine commission ordained, is the administration of such rites (the
Christian sacraments) as are essentially different from
sacrifice; and the *instruction* of the people; an office not
especially allotted to the Jewish priests, but rather to the
whole of the Levites; and so little appropriated even to
them, that persons of any other tribe* were allowed to
teach publicly in the synagogues.

It deserves then to be kept in mind,

I. That Priest, in the two senses just noticed, does
not merely denote two *different* things, but is, strictly
speaking, *equivocal.* The word "house," for instance,
is not equivocal when applied to the houses of the ancients and to our own, though the two are considerably
different; because both are the same *in that which the
word "house" denotes;* viz. in being "a building for
man's habitation:" on the other hand, the word "pub-
lican" in its ordinary sense, and in that in which it
occurs in our version of the New Testament, is equivocal, though in each case it denotes a *man* in a certain
profession in life; because the professions indicated in
each case respectively, by that term, are essentially dif-

---

* As, for instance, Jesus himself, who was of the tribe of Judah, and Paul,
of the tribe of Benjamin.

ferent. And the same is the case with the word priest,
in the two senses now under consideration.

II. That though there is in the Romish Church a
pretended sacrifice, offered by a pretended priest, (in the
other sense,) this creates no just objection to what has
been said; since their practice in this point is a manifest
corruption of Christianity, totally unsupported by any
warrant of Scripture, and manifestly at variance with
the whole spirit of the Gospel; and what we are speaking of is the religion as originally instituted, not, as
subsequently depraved.

III. That the peculiarity in question, as well as every
other of any consequence, affords a strong presumption of
the truth of the religion; and this, independent of any
question as to the *excellence* of the peculiarity. For
either an impostor or an enthusiast would have been
almost sure, on such a point, to fall in with the prevailing
notions and expectations of men; as experience shews,
in the case of such a multitude of different systems of
religion which confessedly have emanated from the
sources alluded to. It cannot be deemed an insignificant
circumstance that the Christian religion should *differ
from all others in a point in which, amidst their infinite
varieties, they all agree.*

IV. That the charge of *Priestcraft,* so often brought
indiscriminately against all religions, by those whose
hostility is in fact directed against Christianity, falls entirely to the ground, when applied, not to the corrup-
tions of the Romish Church, (which certainly does lie
open to the imputation,) but to the religion of the Gospel, as founded on the writings of its promulgators. It

is a religion which has no Priest on earth, no mortal Intercessor to stand between God and his worshippers; but which teaches its votaries to apply, for themselves, to their great and divine High Priest, and to "come boldly to the throne of grace, that they may find help in time of need." Nor are the Christian ministers appointed, as the infidel would insinuate, for the purpose of keeping the people in darkness, but expressly for the purpose of *instructing* them in their religion.

V. Lastly, that Christians should be warned, if they would conform to the design of the Author of their faith, not to think of *substituting* the religion of the minister for their own; his office being, according to Christ's institution, not to serve God instead of them, but to teach and lead them to serve Him themselves.

THE END.

BAXTER, PRINTER, OXFORD.

www.ingramcontent.com/pod-product-compliance
Lightning Source LLC
Chambersburg PA
CBHW080550090426
42735CB00016B/3196